# LEADING
## AS SONS &
## DAUGHTERS

### DISCOVER THE JOY OF
### EMPOWERING OTHERS

**WENDY MANN**

malcolm down

PUBLISHING

First published 2019 by Malcolm Down Publishing Ltd.
www.malcolmdown.co.uk

British Library Cataloguing in Publication Data
A catalogue record for this book is available from the British Library.

ISBN 978-1-912863-06-8

Cover design by NARKAN Ltd

Printed in the UK by Bell & Bain Ltd, Glasgow

# WHAT OTHER PEOPLE ARE SAYING...

Wendy Mann is extremely anointed in leadership! Her new book, *Leading as Sons and Daughters*, is a powerful and practical resource for every believer. Through personal storytelling, Wendy shares her journey of walking out her identity as a child of God in order to learn to lead like Jesus. This book meets you wherever you are in your process of leadership so you can empower others from an internal place of rest. You will walk away with a greater sense of security in your own identity, keys for kingdom leadership, and inspiration to empower those around you to flourish!

If you're a believer who wants to grow in leading in your church, your business, or your family, then this book will activate you to confidently help your people thrive!

*Kris Vallotton*, leader at Bethel Church in Redding, CA, co-founder of Bethel School of Supernatural Ministry, author of thirteen books, including *The Supernatural Ways of Royalty*, *Heavy Rain* and *Poverty, Riches and Wealth*

Wendy is a courageous leader who has over many years modelled authentically and powerfully what it means to lead together as men and women in the church today. She has a long track record of helping people come into freedom, and seeing her grow into the person she has become today has been a huge privilege for me. I'm so grateful for the steps she has taken on the journey and the passion she carries to make the church what it is. Her stamp is very much on our church and we would not be where we are without her contribution. I know you will be blessed by this book, so read and enjoy and bask in the revelation of a woman who has certainly been with Jesus.

*Simon Holley*, Catalyst team leader, senior leader at King's Arms Church, Bedford, UK and author of *Sustainable Power*

If I had to choose one person to write and teach on leading as a son or daughter, it would be my friend Wendy Mann. Wendy has written this brilliant book, not from theoretical principle, but from a life forged in the red-hot love of the Father. Wendy has lived and modelled this book to many hundreds of people who are different because they encountered God through her. This book will challenge, provoke, inspire and reveal God to you. You were born to change the world and do it knowing you are God's special treasure. This book could change your life! Read it and then live it!

*Phil Wilthew*, senior leader at King's Arms Church, Bedford, UK and author of *Developing Prophetic Culture* and *Multiplying Disciples*

I have had the privilege of living with Wendy, receiving ministry from her and serving alongside her in different seasons. In each setting I have found her passionate pursuit of Jesus and her unwavering commitment to be all that she was made to be, both constant and courageous. I wholeheartedly recommend this book to you – it is one born out of practice and is all the better for it. What a joy to see a leader who is so open-handed with that which she has paid such a personal price for. Prepare to be challenged, inspired and empowered as you read.

*Katia Adams*, director of Frequentsee

In any leadership transition there are two major pitfalls that can happen. Leaders can abdicate to try and give the new leader as much space as possible. Or they can stay controlling of what they love and have cherished for years. Wendy is a fantastic example of having stayed clear of both pitfalls as she transitioned her leadership of TSM to me and the rest of the team. Wendy continues to be present in asking good questions and giving of herself without being controlling of my decisions or leadership style. This requires security in identity and consistent obedience to God's voice. I have never experienced transition like Wendy has modelled. It has provided me and the TSM team with a platform to succeed, which I think is the true mark of a good leader. If you succeed alone, you are building a career. If others succeed around you, you are building a legacy. I can't recommend Wendy highly enough. She has truly fought for leading from identity and it's evident every day that we work together.

*Marco Weening*, leader of TSM team at King's Arms Church, Bedford, UK

I couldn't wait to read this book by Wendy, as I know she lives what she writes and this makes her work come alive, stirring, challenging and reaching into areas you don't even know need reaching. She uses a combination of teaching and grace that pack a punch as she brings in personal stories that demonstrate exactly the point she's trying to make. Her love of God and people flows throughout the book and this is seen in her leadership style in real life, too. The topic of this book suits her well and so it's with great pleasure that I commend it to you. Read it. You'll be glad you did!

*Angela Kemm*, itinerant prophetic evangelist: Relational Mission family of churches within Newfrontiers

Having worked alongside Wendy for a number of years, I have had first-hand experience of what it's like to be led by this inspiring woman. We have such different leadership styles, yet she has always sought to understand me and as a result has called out the best in me. Wendy is someone who believes in those she leads and she creates environments where you feel free to be yourself. She has the right balance of compassion and love, mixed with a passion to see people be all they are called to be. Sometimes that means you're nudged into places that feel uncomfortable, but it's in these places you find opportunities to grow. I am so grateful for Wendy's input. It has helped to shape me into the leader I am today.

*Philbe Kellett*, TSM pastoral oversight at King's Arms Church, Bedford, UK

This book is dedicated to Angie Simco and Zoe-Joy Harries. Two spiritual mothers in the church who lived this so naturally and left an amazing legacy.

# CONTENTS

# ACKNOWLEDGEMENTS

There are so many people to thank:

TSM team, so much of what I've learned about leading as a daughter has come through leading TSM with you. Thank you for your patience with my many mistakes and for the way you have championed my successes. You were the best team to lead and I feel so much joy that TSM continues to thrive. (Special mention to Philbe who was there from the very beginning – you, maybe more than anyone, have witnessed first-hand my leadership journey. I think it's fair to say I've changed quite a bit!)

Marco, thank you for being the person I could entrust TSM to. Giving away something so precious has been made easier by your passionate pursuit of Jesus and your desire to learn and grow. Thank you for teaching me how to transition well and, in the process, giving me so many great stories for this book. Before you ask, there are no royalties available!

Simon and PJ, thank you for giving me opportunities to lead when I thought and behaved more like an orphan than a daughter. I am so grateful that you saw what God had put in me, even though for a long time it was hidden behind insecurity and fear. Your continued encouragement is such a gift.

Ali, thank you for the hours you have put into reading and re-reading this book. I am blown away that you would put your own book on hold to champion and invest in mine. Your mind is brilliant and your input into this book means it is so much better than it was. More than being grateful for your editing skills, I am grateful for you. Our friendship is one of my best. I love being part of your family.

Mum and Dad, thank you for being the best parents. Thank you for always cheering me on, for loving me unconditionally and for laying your lives down so that I can succeed. You both inspire me so much.

Father God, I am overwhelmed by Your kindness in my life. Thank You for calling a broken and insecure teenager to be Your daughter, and for using this daughter to influence many hundreds of people. I cannot wait to see the full extent of the legacy You have commissioned me to leave. All of it is for Your glory and Your fame.

# TRUE SUCCESS: An Introduction

*True success isn't what you accomplish in your lifetime, true success is based on what your descendants (or those you pour into) accomplish because of you.*

Bill Johnson[1]

I don't have any children of my own but as a leader I am called to empower and release many 'sons' and 'daughters' around the world. I get so much pleasure from investing in the people around me. When the people I lead grow in their calling and step into their destiny, I know I am achieving what I was put on the earth to do. God's Kingdom comes with great effectiveness when His people actually believe who He says they are. Churches, workplaces and whole communities can be transformed when Christians are encouraged and released by the leaders around them. More and more my leadership is about pouring into the people I develop so that they grasp their significance and thrive in all God's called them to.

The whole point of this book is to see leaders freed up to champion the people they invest in. I want to inspire and equip leaders to be the best they can be, so that those they lead flourish and succeed. God has dealt with huge amounts of fear and insecurity in my leadership. These are increasingly being replaced with faith and confidence. I have discovered the joy of empowering others and I want to enable other leaders to do the same.

Many of you have been leading for years but, like me, you recognise there is so much more to learn when it comes to leading like Jesus. My prayer is that this book will give you fresh vision and tools for the legacy God has called you to leave. Others of you wouldn't yet consider yourself a leader, but calling out the greatness in others is something you aspire to. The truth is, whether you have an official leadership role or not, all of us are called to influence the people around us. John Maxwell, a highly respected leadership expert, points out that even the most isolated individual will influence 10,000 other people during their lifetime.[2] If this isn't compelling enough, Jesus Himself has entrusted us with the mandate to make disciples of all nations. All of us have been commissioned to make disciples who make disciples. All of us have the privilege of shaping our church, our family, and our workplace by investing in the people around us. Whether you would call yourself a leader or not you are going to influence a vast number of people throughout your lifetime. The vital question for all of us to ask is, how are we going to use the influence we have?

A crucial part of my leadership journey has been learning to recognise where my thinking and behaviour is limiting myself and those around me. The ultimate goal in godly leadership is to grow in revelation of your sonship and daughterhood so that your leadership flows out of this place of security. People under this kind of secure leadership have the potential to accomplish breathtaking things for God.

How are you going to use the influence you have? My aim throughout the rest of this book is to demonstrate what sons and daughters look like when they lead, and give us tools to increasingly lead out of that identity. I want to motivate us to change the way we think so that the people we have the privilege of investing in become the best they can be. I like to imagine what churches, families and workplaces would look like if we used our influence to prefer the people around us; if we followed Jesus' example in laying our lives down to make others great. I think God's Kingdom would advance in remarkable ways. Let's go on a journey together of learning how to lead as sons and daughters. Let's discover the joy of empowering others.

# 1. SONS AND DAUGHTERS

God told me very clearly to stay on the floor.

We were coming to the end of a worship time at TSM³ and I was about to speak to our students about spiritual parenting; about how they could lay down their lives to empower and release the people around them. I was in the process of handing over leadership of the evening school to Marco who was hosting the meeting that night. I had been leading TSM for seven years by this point and God had spoken multiple times about passing the baton to others. This was the last talk I was going to do as leader of the school and I was looking forward to seeing what God would do.

God really met with us during worship and I lay down on the floor to enjoy His presence. Marco and I had talked before the evening started about the time I would like to be on my feet to speak. I was aware that our agreed time was fast approaching so I started to think about getting up so I could prompt Marco to bring worship to a close. It was at this moment that God clearly told me to stay on the floor. He told me that this was a key moment for Marco in his leadership of TSM and that I was not to get up until he decided, without any prompts from me, to end worship and invite me up to speak.

Marco went to the microphone and told the students he felt we should linger a bit longer in God's presence. On the outside I looked like I was lying on the floor worshipping God and enjoying being with Him, like everybody else. On the inside it was a different story. I was having to consciously fight the urge to get up and take leadership of the evening back from Marco. There was a wrestle going on in my heart. The secure daughter part of me knew it was right to trust Marco to lead, that it was actually a great leadership call to prioritise God's presence in that moment. The insecure orphan part of me, the part of my thinking not yet renewed enough to respond like a daughter, wanted to take back control.

When one of the students started singing a worship song, which meant I would have even less time to speak, the wrestle in my heart intensified. My thinking switched between responding like an orphan and thinking like a daughter.

*'I can't believe this is my last talk as leader of TSM and I am going to have hardly any time to share. I don't feel particularly valued.'*

'This is great, though, because I'm modelling with Marco what I am about to get up and teach.'

*'Maybe Marco is doing this on purpose because he doesn't want me to speak for very long.'*

'Marco isn't like that and even if he was the truth is I don't need long to speak. My security and value is wrapped up in who God says I am, not what I do.'

*'If I just got up Marco would know to end worship.'*

'I can trust Marco's leadership. This is a key moment for him to step into his new role.'

I am so glad my daughterhood won the wrestle in my heart that evening. I stayed on the floor until Marco made the decision to end the time of worship. and it turned out I had more than enough time to share what God had put on my heart. I learned some valuable lessons that night. Firstly, that God is passionate about exposing where I still think like an orphan so I can increasingly believe the truth about who I am as His daughter. Secondly, that growing in revelation of my daughterhood is never going to be a done deal, it is a lifelong journey and there will always be more for me to discover. Thirdly, that being secure in my identity is crucial if I want to release and empower those I lead to be everything God has called them to be.

## FATHER AND SON

Jesus modelled the importance of knowing God as His Father and knowing who He was as a dearly loved son. It was the foundation of who He was and from which everything He did flowed. Jesus lived a life of utter dependence on His Father. He regularly withdrew to solitary places to pray. He told the Jewish leaders He could do nothing by Himself, '[the Son] can do only what he sees his Father doing' (John 5:19). Even as a young boy His priority was intimacy with His Father. When Mary and Joseph eventually found Jesus after He had been missing for three days following the Passover festival, He was surprised by their anxiety. '"Why were you searching for me?" he asked. "Didn't you know I had to be in my Father's house?"' (Luke 2:49).

As well as knowing God as His Father, Jesus understood who He was as God's beloved son. Jesus received affirmation of His

7

sonship right at the outset of His ministry. When He came up out of the waters at His baptism, the heavens were torn open, the Holy Spirit descended on Him like a dove and His Father's voice resounded from heaven, 'You are my Son, whom I love; with you I am well pleased' (Mark 1:11). Knowing God as His Father and understanding His identity as a dearly loved son were two sides of the same coin for Jesus. You cannot relate to God as Father like Jesus did unless you know you are a loved child. Equally you cannot know security and complete acceptance in your sonship if you do not understand God is your Father. Revelation of one feeds into and reinforces revelation of the other.

Jesus' leadership flowed out of His sonship; He led as a son. His understanding of God's perfect love for Him and complete acceptance of Him resulted in an internal security that impacted everything. Jesus' sonship enabled Him to resist the temptation of the enemy in the wilderness. It drove Him to be a God pleaser rather than a people pleaser; Jesus was not afraid to confront people when necessary or offend religious leaders by putting people before protocol (Mark 3:1-6). Jesus' confidence in His identity allowed Him to release His disciples to do the things He was doing way before they were ready. It also meant He did not need to grasp for power or recognition from others. Jesus regularly withdrew from the crowds to be with His Father, and a few days before He was crucified Jesus willingly got on His knees to serve His disciples by washing their feet. Jesus is our example when it comes to leadership.

I remember several years ago spending time with Jesus to ask Him about where I belonged as a leader in the church. I was a single woman in my twenties and, to be honest, there was a real lack of women in leadership for me to look to. I had already been leading for a few years and I knew there was a significant leadership call on my life. My issue was that I struggled to know what I should be called, what my leadership title should be. I knew in my family of churches I could not be an elder, which was not a problem for me as I did not want to be one. Yet I did want to know what was possible for me. I asked God what leadership title I should be aiming towards; what was He calling me to be?

God's answer was immediate and clear. He told me that the only title He wanted me to focus on in my leadership was daughter; that this was the title I should aim towards. God told me if I did that, if I spent the rest of my life learning more and more what it means to be His daughter, He would lead me into a spacious place and open up leadership opportunities for me I never dreamt were possible. This is exactly what has happened. As I have focused my attention on being His daughter He has provided amazing opportunities for me to lead and I know there is still so much more to come. Prioritising being a daughter has also transformed how I lead. It has meant I have gone from being very insecure and intense in my leadership to much more confident and releasing. I am obviously still on a journey but the fruit I have seen in other people's lives as a result of prioritising my daughterhood has been amazing.

As Jesus' disciples we are called to follow His example. Knowing God as our Father and knowing who we are as His beloved sons and daughters is the most important journey for us to go on throughout our Christian life. It is important first and foremost for us as individuals. Taking leadership out of the equation, we need to know our identity as God's children for our own benefit; so that we can fully enjoy the relationship we have been drafted into with a perfect Father. The fact that we have been adopted by the God of the universe is a mind-blowing, life-altering truth; it changes everything. Growing in understanding of the implications of our adoption is a lifelong journey every believer must go on.

As we go on this journey of enjoying our adoption, of letting the truth of who we are in Christ sink into our hearts, the same internal security Jesus enjoyed becomes available to us. As a result we are able to have the same leadership impact on the people around us that Jesus had on His followers. Growing in revelation of our sonship or daughterhood is crucial for every believer, but it is particularly important for Christians who lead. What we believe about ourselves on the inside will come out of us in the way we interact with and relate to the people we develop. If we lead out of insecurity and fear, we will struggle to really empower the people around us to flourish in God. Conversely, if we lead out of security we will be able to provide a springboard for those we lead to be everything God has called them to be. Like Jesus, we are called to lead as sons and daughters. In order to do that we need to win the tussle that is going on for our identity.

## ORPHAN TO HEIR

Have you ever found yourself in a position where you have done something wrong, and even in the moment you knew it was wrong but you did it anyway? I remember an occasion when I found a particular leadership meeting hard. I must have made it obvious in the meeting because later the same day one of my elders approached me to ask if I was OK. He wondered if I had been upset in the meeting. Even though just a couple of hours earlier I had been crying with Jesus about the conversation I had found difficult, I heard myself telling the leader that I was fine. I lied to my leader and I knew exactly what I was doing.

This is a brilliant example of the internal tussle that often takes place between our old orphan way of thinking and behaving and our new way of responding as loved and secure sons and daughters. The truth is that it's not in my nature to lie. As a cherished daughter of God I can take off my mask and be honest about my feelings with my leaders and the people around me. Even if people misunderstand me or struggle to empathise with me, the truth is God always understands and He always protects. In this instance my old orphan thinking – the fear of what my leader would think and the potential of rejection and humiliation – shouted louder than my daughterhood. The result was that I lied in order to protect myself. I apologised to my leader the next morning and spent time with God repenting for where my thinking had not yet caught up with my identity in Christ.

The truth is that before we gave our lives to Jesus all of us lived as spiritual orphans. We were separated from the relationship we were created for, disconnected from our Father and slaves to fear and shame. The second we said yes to Jesus our identity was completely transformed. In an instant we became dearly loved sons and daughters. John puts it this way, 'See what great love the Father has lavished on us, that we should be called children of God!

And that is what we are!' (1 John 3:1). We have been adopted into God's family with a perfect Heavenly Father and a victorious older brother. We are no longer orphans but heirs of God and co-heirs with Christ. We are no longer slaves to fear, we are slaves to righteousness. We are beloved sons and daughters of the God of the universe and nothing can change this reality. Our adoption is a done deal.

Yet often our minds are on a journey of catching up with the truth about what has happened to our hearts. In Romans 12:2 Paul gives us this instruction, 'be transformed by the renewing of your mind'. Whatever we think about who we are will define how we behave. The battle for our identity really is fought in the mind. Behind orphan behaviour is orphan thinking, and when we recognise it we need to change the way we think. We need to repent for the wrong thinking we have about ourselves or the lies we believe about God and instead choose to intentionally believe the truth. As we do this deliberately and consistently over time, we start to think more like sons and daughters, and as a result our behaviour changes too.

This is such an important journey for us to go on as leaders. The more we are able to lead out of our adoption, the more we have the potential to see those around us flourish in their relationship with God. When we lead like orphans, our thinking and behaviour is rooted in fear and insecurity. Our focus tends to be on how to improve our own sense of self-worth rather than championing people around us. Insecure leaders live for the praise and approval of others. Their significance is wrapped up in their performance so they have a tendency to be risk-averse and feel threatened by those who appear more gifted than them. Orphan-minded leaders want to be seen as strong so they are likely to avoid being honest with those they lead about areas of weakness or struggle. When it comes to confrontation, insecure leaders either avoid it altogether or they can be overly harsh with what they say. People under this kind of leadership are likely to feel insecure themselves and as a result their potential in God will be limited.

In contrast, when we lead as sons and daughters our main aim is to see the people we develop overtake and outrun us. In fact, we are eager to give away all that God has done in us so that those we are investing in are fast-tracked in their relationship with Him. When we lead out of our identity, our thinking and behaviour is rooted in faith and security. Knowing how loved and accepted we are by the God of the universe focuses our attention on how to give that love and acceptance away to others. This results in leadership that is sacrificial and releasing, where our main priority is to lift others up rather than seek recognition for ourselves. Secure leaders are comfortable with mistakes and they champion risk. They do not shy away from confronting people when they need to, but they do so with genuine love in their heart for the person in front of them. Leaders who know who they are follow the example of Christ; they lay down their lives to promote and champion others. When you are under this kind of leadership, anything is possible.

This seems like a big ask for those of us in leadership. Hopefully it will be an encouragement to hear that leading out of our identity in Christ is a process and it takes time. The reality is that most of our thinking and behaviour are a mix of renewed son-ship thoughts and old orphan mindsets. The hope over time is that our renewed thinking more regularly trumps our fears and insecurities; that as Scripture promises, we will be transformed as we renew our minds. This is not always going to be a linear progression. It is possible to be doing really well at being a son or daughter in a particular area of leadership, but then find yourself in another context where God wants to take the truth deeper. Much like my experience when God told me to stay on the floor during worship. I would not have described myself as a controlling leader at the time, but God used the situation to expose a bit more orphan thinking so I could step into greater freedom.

## OPPORTUNITIES EVERYWHERE

As you go on this journey of growing in revelation of your identity, you will discover that there are opportunities everywhere for you to renew your mind. God is very committed to putting His finger on orphan thinking and behaviour so that we can increasingly live in the truth of who we are in Christ. He does it first and foremost for our own relationship with Him, so that we can enjoy all the benefits of knowing Him as a perfect Father and knowing who we are as dearly loved children. He also does it so we can have the best kind of influence on the world around us and those we invest in. Jesus saw many disciples empowered and released to have influence wherever they went. He wants the same for the people we lead today and His plan is to do it through you and me.

Often opportunities God gives us to renew our mind will not come about directly through our leadership, but rather through our day-to-day relationship with Him. I had a very clear orphan response recently when a friend of mine was given a large sum of money from her family to help her buy a house. I had been looking into buying a house myself and had met with a financial advisor to work out my money situation. I had a bit of a deposit I had been saving over many years but I was going to need a miracle in order to get on the property ladder, so I began to pray. Maybe a month after I started asking God for money, my friend received her gift. It was more than the deposit I had saved and she had done nothing to earn it.

I told God in no uncertain terms that I thought He had got it wrong when it came to this particular blessing. I was offended that my friend now had more money than me even though I had been saving for years and she had saved very little. This was not fair! It was obvious from my response that this was an area of my thinking where I was still operating like an orphan. The miracle my friend experienced made me feel like I had missed out, that God did not want to bless me as much as he wanted to bless her. Of course, a daughter responds very differently. A daughter is able to celebrate when those around her are blessed because she understands it takes nothing away from the blessing God has for her. A daughter understands that she has access to all the resources of heaven; she knows there is enough money to go round for her and her friends. A daughter remains secure in her Father's love for her, both when her prayers are answered and when they seem unanswered.

I took some time with Jesus to repent for my orphan thinking in this situation and to intentionally think differently about money and provision. I thanked God for the way He had blessed my friend and asked Him to bless her with even more provision. I then asked Him again for myself, thanking Him that He knew what I needed and trusting Him for the journey He had me on. Once I got past the initial offence this became a wonderful opportunity for me to renew my mind and step more fully into my identity as a daughter. The opportunity did not come through a leadership situation, but I know it will help me to lead more effectively as a daughter. The freedom Jesus brought me I am now able to pass on to others. The journey out of orphan thinking and into security is more up and down than it is linear, but every time we take hold of an opportunity God gives us to renew our mind we take a step closer to leading like Jesus did.

## LEADING AS SONS AND DAUGHTERS

I talk about leading like an orphan or out of insecurity a lot throughout this book. When I do I am referring to the parts of our thinking, and therefore behaviour, which have not yet caught up with the spiritual reality of our adoption in Christ. As we have seen already, our leadership is often a mix of orphan and sonship thinking and behaviour. We have a lifelong journey to go on of renewing our minds, so that we can increasingly live out of the truth of our identity as sons and daughters. As we follow Jesus and He leads us into freedom, there are things we can do to position ourselves for greater revelation of this truth. I want to focus on and unpack just two simple practices, which will enable the secure part of our thinking to become louder than the lies and fear that try to keep us trapped.

1) Pursue intimacy with the Father

Growing in our sonship and daughterhood is not about trying really hard. You cannot strive and strain to more clearly understand your adoption. It is a work of the Holy Spirit. The apostle Paul puts it this way: 'The Spirit you received does not make you slaves, so that you live in fear again; rather, the Spirit you received brought about your adoption to sonship. And by him we cry, 'Abba, Father.' The Spirit himself testifies with our spirit that we are God's children' (Romans 8:15-16). In other words, it is the Holy Spirit in us who enables us to relate to God as our Father. It is also the Holy Spirit who reveals to us the reality of our adoption as sons and daughters. The multifaceted truth about who we are as dearly loved children is too incomprehensible for our brains to understand. We need revelation from the Holy Spirit that bypasses our brain and goes straight to our heart.

In practice this looks like carving out time to pursue intimacy with the Father, just like Jesus did. It looks like asking the Holy Spirit to give you fresh revelation on a regular basis of who God is as your Father and who you are as His child. It looks like meditating on truth in Scripture about the nature of God and our new creation identity and asking the Holy Spirit to make the truth come alive. When the Holy Spirit breathes on truth it moves from theory and head knowledge to reality through encounter and experience. I think one of the key dangers for leaders is being with the Father for the sake of those they are leading and where they are leading them, rather than for the love and joy of their own relationship with Him. We spend time with Jesus in order to have success in our ministry or workplace, to write a great preach or to seek God for next steps for those we are investing in. Of course these things are important to go to Jesus with, but we must prioritise intimacy with God first and foremost because *we* want to grow in intimacy with Him as sons and daughters.

As we pursue intimacy with the Father He will speak to us and reveal truth to us, which will help us to grow in our sonship and daughterhood. Recently, God has been speaking to me about what love looks like through the well-known passage in 1 Corinthians 13. I have been thoroughly challenged personally about the way I love people, recognising how far I often fall short of the standard Paul sets in this scripture. Much of the reason why I struggle to love people sacrificially is because of my old orphan thinking. It is difficult not to envy others when you think their blessing somehow takes away blessing from you. It is difficult to be patient with people around you when you do not understand God's patience with you. It is only as we grow in revelation of our adoption and how sacrificially the Father loves us that we are able to give His love away to others.

So in this season, as the Father is provoking me to love more like Him, I am pursuing intimacy with the one who loves perfectly. I am asking God to fill me more and more with His love for me so that I experience it tangibly. I am trusting as I go on this journey of pursuing greater intimacy with the Father and receiving His unconditional love for me that what He does in me will ultimately flow out of me. My motivation for receiving His love is first and foremost for me, so I comprehend at a deeper level how He feels about me as His daughter. I also know that what I receive I get to give away to others, so I am expecting my personal journey to also have an impact on my leadership. How are you doing at pursuing intimacy with the Father because you are hungry to know Him more personally? What does God want to reveal to you and do in you so that you grow in revelation of your adoption in Christ?

2) Commit to the journey of renewing your mind

The progression from orphan to dearly loved child takes place primarily in our thinking. Our adoption is a done deal, but our thinking takes time to adjust to this new spiritual reality. If we want to increasingly think and lead like sons and daughters, we have to commit to embracing the journey of renewing our minds; of making the most of the opportunities God gives us to recognise wrong thinking and choose instead to agree with the truth.

The biggest challenge for me personally with this has been intentionally choosing to think like a daughter after I have recognised orphan thinking. The way I am wired means I can fairly easily identify when my thinking or behaviour does not match up with my daughterhood. The challenge is to not stop at knowing where I need to change but to actually take the time to adjust my thinking. Repentance means to change the way you think. It is not just saying sorry, which is how many Christians define it, it is choosing to deliberately think differently. This takes time and intentionality.

When I expressed my disappointment to Jesus about my friend being given more money than I had saved, I had the opportunity to renew my mind. Repentance in this instance started with acknowledging where I was thinking like an orphan. I told God I was sorry for thinking that my friend being blessed meant there was less blessing available for me, and I apologised for responding with jealousy and offence. Then I worked out how I needed to think differently, based on my daughterhood. I thanked God that He never runs out of blessings and that when others are blessed I can celebrate. I thanked God that He is my provider and that I can trust His ability to know and provide exactly what I need. I then prayed for financial breakthrough for my situation with renewed faith because of my changed perspective.

In some cases when you renew your mind you change the way you think and it is a done deal, your thinking never slips back into its old ways again. I think more often than not we have to keep intentionally choosing to believe the truth God has shown us. Sometimes I have made the decision to look at myself in the mirror every morning over a period of weeks to speak truth to myself. My old ways of thinking have been so ingrained that I have had to persistently fight to change my thoughts. As I have waged war against my wrong thinking by regularly declaring the truth, bit by bit my thinking has changed. When we commit to the journey of renewing our minds and are intentional about meditating on the truth, we are increasingly able to live as sons and daughters.

Sometimes our orphan thinking is attached to pain we have experienced in our lives. Even though we are renewing our mind, we might struggle to break our old orphan responses. In these instances it is helpful to take time with Jesus and trusted friends to seek freedom from the pain our orphan thinking is attached to. We might need to express our pain to God and go through the process of forgiving people who have hurt us. Seeking God for internal freedom and intentionally believing truth is a powerful combination when it comes to renewing your mind and living out of your new identity. How are you doing at recognising and embracing the opportunities God is giving you to renew your mind? Are you being intentional about recognising orphan thinking and then making time to work out how you need to think differently? Committing to the journey of renewing our minds is a key part in the process of us changing from orphans to heirs.

If we want to lead like Jesus we need to lead as sons and daughters. Sons and daughters know an internal security, which motivates them to champion and release the people they lead in a way that orphans cannot. When we lead as sons and daughters, we create a spacious place for people around us to flourish. We have the privilege of seeing those we empower come alive as we give them courage to believe they are who God says they are and they can do what He says they can do. There is something very special about seeing the people you are developing overtake and outrun you.

Throughout the rest of this book I will unpack the impact of leading as adopted children versus leading out of our old orphan thinking. I want to motivate us to prioritise our sonship and daughterhood in our own relationship with God and in our leadership. The chapters are likely to reveal aspects of your thinking that are yet to be renewed and so characteristics of your leadership that are still rooted in orphan mindsets. They are not intended to be used as sticks to beat yourself up with where you identify mistakes you have made: that would be an orphan response. Instead, the chapters are intended to reveal the kind of leadership possible for all believers who are committed to pursuing intimacy with God as their Father.

Of course, no leader will ever be perfect; there will always be more for us to learn, which is a good thing. I sent one of my draft chapters from this book to a friend of mine in the States. She sent me a message after she had read it encouraging me in my leadership and telling me she would love the opportunity to be led by me for a season. I quickly replied to remind her I was nowhere near perfect and that I still make many mistakes as I lead. I found her reply thoroughly helpful and releasing. She said, 'I know, but that's what makes it all the more attractive. Seriously, it would be hard to follow a perfect leader.'

As you read this book, take comfort from the fact that you will never be perfect in your leadership. Get good at apologising when your old orphan thinking takes precedent and realise that your mistakes actually make you easier to follow. Try not to see the descriptions of secure leadership as simply behaviours you need to work hard to adopt as you lead. The truth is that if we only focus on changing our behaviour without transforming on the inside, any changes we do see will not be sustainable and will not last. Instead, can I invite you to commit to learning more about what it means to know God as your Father and who He says you are as His dearly loved son or daughter? Let God pour His love into your heart, let Him speak truth to you so that you can renew your mind. Then let what He does inside of you come out of you as you lead. It is time to embrace the journey of learning to lead as sons and daughters.

# 2. DO YOU KNOW WHO YOU ARE?

I remember writing training material for a day away with some of our key leaders at King's Arms. The plan was to help us understand ourselves better so that we could more effectively draw the best out of others. Topics on the agenda included listening well and asking good questions, as well as understanding the different ways people learn and how they receive encouragement. I was going to speak about the importance of completing tasks and loving people with excellence. In my experience, some leaders lean more towards completing tasks with excellence but miss opportunities to love people in the process. Other leaders veer more towards neglecting tasks that have to be done because they prioritise others' feelings and wellbeing above getting the job done. My aim was to illustrate both ends of the spectrum so that our leaders could work out which way they leaned and whether they needed to make any changes to grow their leadership gift.

I already knew that my tendency was to lean more towards completing tasks, especially if I felt under pressure. If I was in the middle of doing work that felt challenging, or if I was running out of time to get something done, I would struggle to acknowledge people if they walked into my office. My default would be to keep my head down and avoid eye contact to communicate that I did not want to be interrupted. The positive side to this was that I always did a good job when it came to completing my work. The negative side was that people I led and colleagues around me did not always feel loved and valued by me. As it happened, knowing this about myself really paid off as I was writing my training material.

I felt fairly stressed as I was doing my prep and I was quickly running out of time. I decided to sit in our church coffee shop with headphones in to communicate clearly that I was not to be disturbed. As I was writing about the importance of getting a healthy balance between completing tasks and loving people, I felt a tap on my shoulder. A colleague of mine who I rarely have the chance to catch up with had stopped to say hello. I consciously felt the internal pull to settle for a brief acknowledgement before turning back to my computer, but I knew I needed to give her some quality time. I took my headphones out, lowered my laptop screen and spent a chunk of time in conversation with my friend. My self-awareness in this instance enabled me to lean away from being task-driven in order to really love the person in front of me.

Of course, most of us aren't exclusively at one end of this spectrum. Most of us slide up and down the scale depending on the situation we are in and how we are doing. What I have come to understand is that growing in self-awareness is vital if we want to be leaders who enable people around us to thrive. When we understand who we are, how we think and the way we see the world, we can be aware of potential vulnerable spots in our leadership and take steps to limit them. When we know our strengths and weaknesses, we can build team around us to complement our strengths and balance out our weaknesses. When we are able to recognise what we are feeling and what our emotions are telling us, we are more likely to be able to stay healthy in our leadership and lead others into freedom. If we embrace the journey of getting to know ourselves, we will be quicker to identify and do away with orphan thinking and behaviour. As a result, we will be able to more wholeheartedly receive our sonship or daughterhood. It is helpful for all of us to be asking the question, do I really know who I am?

## GROWING IN SELF-AWARENESS

A potential danger of going on this journey of self-awareness is becoming overly analytical of who you are and how you are growing. If you are not careful, your journey into sonship or daughterhood can become a self-improvement programme rather than being led by the Spirit. The truth is that Jesus is responsible for sanctifying us. He is thoroughly committed to our growth and development. He is the one leading us; our job is to learn to follow Him really closely. Having said that, we do have a responsibility to partner with what God wants to do in us, so we become all He calls us to be. If we remain ignorant about who we are and how our behaviour impacts people around us, our effectiveness as leaders will be limited. Equally, if we stay passive when God reveals areas of our lives He wants to change, our relationship with Him will stagnate. Our aim should be to walk the middle road of letting God initiate our growth, but making the choice to respond wholeheartedly to Him when He does.

God has taught me so much about myself over my years of

leadership. Some lessons I have learned more quickly than others and I am aware that there is still much more learning to come. Each lesson has taught me more about what it means to be a daughter and how I can increasingly lead in a way that draws the best out of me and those around me. God has made us all unique, and the lessons He wants us to learn will be different for each one of us. A life-defining moment of growing in self-awareness for me might have little relevance to you because we are wired different-ly. Each of us has our own journey to go on with God. We must fight the temptation to compare ourselves to others, wishing we were more like them rather than who God has uniquely made us to be. We must also remain humble and teachable, able and willing to learn from anyone and everyone and whatever circum-stances or situations the Father leads us into. Let me unpack some of the key lessons I have learned about myself over the years that have grown me as a daughter and a leader.

1) Reflective thinker

Some people know what they think about things straight away. They hear about a particular situation or they are asked a specif-ic question and they know immediately what to say. People like this used to intimidate me, especially when they said what they thought with confidence and conviction. I assumed that because I was not as certain about what I thought, they must be right; that they had the right answer and I just needed to catch up. The result of this assumption was that I rarely took time to work out what I really thought or to value and communicate my opinion. Mix this with the orphan tendency to want to please people and you end up agreeing with things you actually disagree with and doing things God has not asked you to do.

God has taught me over the years that I am a reflective thinker – that I communicate what is in my heart most effectively when I have had time to mull over what I think. I am one of those people who can come away from a conversation and a few hours later work out the thing I really wanted to say. I reflect on question and answer sessions and suddenly realise how I could have brilliantly responded to a question I had no clue how to answer in the moment. In these instances I have had to learn to lean into Jesus and trust Him to speak to me and guide me. It has been a great way of growing my dependence on God. It is not always possible to have reflection time when you lead.

In other instances, when reflection time is possible, I have learned to take it before I share my opinion. If I am asked to take on new responsibility or make an important work decision, I communicate that I need time to deliberate before responding. As I have grown in my security as a daughter, I have sometimes taken opportunities to go back to my team when my thinking has changed as a result of chewing on what I had previously said. Understanding that I am a reflective thinker means that I no longer keep quiet when others sound confident. I recognise that although what I think and feel may take longer to formulate, it is just as valuable and important as other voices in the mix. Where historically I may have taken on responsibility that did not fit or bring me life, now I take time to ask Jesus what to say yes and no to, which in turn makes me more effective in my calling and leadership.

2) Pause to celebrate

I am a pioneer by nature and I love starting new things. Doing things that people have not done before gives me life. We need leaders in the church and the marketplace who are pioneers. People who refuse to just settle for what has always been and instead create new paths and opportunities for people to explore and enjoy. My passion to pioneer is a great strength but, as with any strength, it also has its weaknesses. One of the main weaknesses of a pioneer is the tendency to rush on to the next new thing without taking sufficient time to pause and really celebrate what God has done. When we forget to celebrate, we miss the opportunity to give God all the glory for what has happened. One of the dangers with this is that it can inadvertently lead us into self-reliance; tempting us to believe that our success was all down to us. When we neglect celebration we also bypass the chance to really value and thank the people who have been involved in partnering with us and God to see breakthrough.

As God has taught me these things about myself I have been able to be intentional about pausing to really celebrate what He is doing, without watering down my desire to see more. I have learned to consciously champion and thank God for the people serving alongside me, whilst holding that in tension with seeing how they could grow in God and wanting that for them. When I visit churches, my natural default is often to see the things that could be developed and changed because I know God wants more for His bride. Yet I am learning how to hold on to the dream while prioritising encouraging leaders and celebrating what God is already doing.

As a pioneer I am always wanting more; more of God, more from Him and more for the people I am championing. God is teaching me that celebration is often the launch pad for the more I am longing for. As I am pausing to celebrate, it is teaching me more about being a daughter and reminding me of my complete dependence on God. This, in turn, is making my ability to pioneer more effective because I am looking to Jesus for success rather than relying on my own ability. Celebrating also communicates love and value to the people I lead. It shows them that they are not just a cog in a machine: a means to an end to get a job done. Rather, they are an important part of the body. We are all family together, learning to be sons and daughters who follow their Father really closely.

## 3) Stay connected

I have often withdrawn from people if I feel like I have upset them or if they have upset me. As I have grown in my identity as a daughter I have learned that withdrawing is an orphan response. It is often rooted in the fear of being rejected and usually stems deep down from a rejection of oneself. Withdrawing is an orphan's way of protecting themselves from further rejection. The problem with withdrawing is that it results in a breakdown of relationships and it hinders people's ability to work in team. God is passionate about healthy relationships and team is really important to Him – look at the Trinity. Recognising my tendency to withdraw has provoked me to go on a journey of breaking agreement with lies I believed about myself so that I can increasingly know and enjoy God's acceptance. The result is that I am more able to choose to stay connected with friends and colleagues and work through relational challenges, even when it feels costly.

I remember a key moment when I chose connection over withdrawal with one of our elders. I was preaching about Jesus one Sunday and had agreed with the elder hosting the meeting that I would preach first so that we could have worship in the second half of the meeting as a response. I really felt God was in the decision and I was very expectant for what He would do among us. A few days before the Sunday, I had a call from the elder hosting to say that the plan would need to be changed because of an important announcement that needed to be made. I managed to hold myself together on the phone before bursting into tears as soon as I hung up. I was gutted.

My orphan default would have been to say nothing more about the conversation, to just work through my disappointment on my own with Jesus and move on. I knew, however, if I was not honest with this elder about how I really felt, I would be tempted to withdraw from him and that would negatively impact our relationship. So I called him back. The conversation was not particularly articulate on my part. I cried as I spoke and nothing changed with regard to the Sunday plan. Yet my daughterhood went to a whole new level. Being honest about my disappointment and being met with so much grace meant that I stayed open and connected with my friend. It was a breakthrough moment for me.

Sons and daughters are able to stay connected and present in relationships, even when there are challenges, because they know they are completely accepted by God. Their security in His love means they can lean into relationships rather than withdrawing from them. This has had a huge impact on my leadership. It means I am increasingly able to model Jesus to the people around me by pursuing connection even when others choose to withdraw. Jesus' priority is always to pursue relationship even if we reject and turn our backs on Him. What do your relationships with others reveal about how much you are living in the truth of your identity?

These are just some of the ways God has taught me about who I am and how I tick. At times it has been a bumpy journey, but as I have grown in self-awareness in these areas I have been able to start identifying and changing orphan thinking. I have been able to lean away from the broken parts of my leadership and lean into and celebrate the ways that I lead as a daughter. God is committed to making us more like Jesus as we follow Him. An essential part of this process is recognising how He is getting our attention when He wants to mould us into the likeness of His son. What is God revealing to you in this season about who you are and the way you are wired? If it is something to celebrate, then make the most of thanking God for the strengths and gifts He has given you. If it is something that requires you to change the way you think so that you increasingly live out of your identity, maybe you need to commit to going on that journey with your Father. Growing in self-awareness is crucial if we want to be all God has called us to be and help others do the same.

## EMOTIONAL HEALTH

An integral part of a person's journey into self-awareness is their pursuit of emotional health.

Scripture portrays Jesus as one who had intense, raw, emotional experiences and was able to express his emotions in unashamed, unembarrassed freedom to others. He did not repress or project his feelings onto others. Instead, we read of Jesus responsibly experiencing the full range of human emotion throughout his earthly ministry.[4]

I love this about Jesus. What a man! He was strong yet gentle, full of authority yet completely humble, and on every step of His ministry journey He allowed Himself to feel really deeply. Jesus wept at Lazarus' grave (John 11:35), He was furious at the corruption in the Temple (John 2:13-17), He had compassion for widows (Luke 7:13) and emotional longing to be with His disciples (Luke 22:15). Jesus models for us what being emotionally healthy as a son and also as a leader looks like. I wonder how we are doing at following His example?

Emotions are a gift from God to us. They are not meant to be feared, held at arm's length or overanalysed. When we feel emotion and express it in a healthy way we look like our Heavenly Father. Emotions enable us to feel fully alive on the inside because when we are emotionally healthy our hearts are awake. When we feel deeply we are also more able to represent the Father to the people around us and see them enjoy freedom. I still vividly remember the first time a friend of mine cried with me when I was expressing pain about something I was going through. It was at a time in my life when I was just beginning to learn about my feelings and what was going on in my heart. My default response to my tears was to try to shut them down as quickly as possible because I felt embarrassed and weak. When I saw tears rolling down my friend's face as she responded to the pain in my heart it was completely overwhelming. I had never experienced that level of compassion directed towards me before. My friend's tears gave me permission to express my pain and gave me a glimpse into God's love and compassion for me. It was a significant turning point in realising that my emotions were actually a gift.

As is often the case with these things, there is a spectrum when it comes to being emotionally healthy, with two extremes we need to avoid and a middle road it is important that we aim for. On one end of the spectrum, it is possible for people to be ruled by their emotions. What they feel is so overwhelming and all-consuming that it trumps the truth written in Scripture. It is true that emotions are a gift from God, but we cannot live our lives letting what we feel control us. I am not at the extreme end of being ruled by my emotion, but these days I am definitely more connected than I am shut down. I can feel a whole host of emotions throughout the course of a day, and sometimes multiple emotions in a single moment. The truth is that I cannot let my emotions dictate choices I make, the way I interact with others or what I believe. Emotions are a brilliant servant but they are a terrible master.

The emotions we feel are a great way to identify what is going on in our hearts and they are crucial in enabling us to access freedom. They also help us to understand more fully where God has called us to have influence. Often it is situations that evoke compassion or anger in us that God has gifted us to change. Yet the truth we read in Scripture about who God is and who we are, about the hope we have and the victory we live in, will never change. The truth is unchanging, no matter what is going on in our lives or how we feel in our hearts. Our emotions must always be subject to the truth, so that it's the truth that defines and guides us. When we refuse to let our emotions muddy the truth in God's Word we are able to encourage others to build their lives on the truth too.

The other end of the spectrum sees people emotionally shut down. The emphasis here can be so focused on doggedly believing and holding on to the truth that a person's emotions are sidelined. Emotions can be seen as deceptive and unpredictable and so people rarely take the time to even look below the surface at how they feel. Sadly, people who live like this miss out on the gift of feeling how Jesus feels. They cannot weep with those who weep, which means they also struggle to rejoice with those who rejoice. This is not the fullness of life that God promises us. He has so much more for us than an emotional flatline.

When someone is shut down emotionally they are not immune to emotion, nor are they unaffected by pain when they face difficult circumstances. The difference between someone who is emotionally healthy and someone who is not is what they do with what they feel. If we neglect to acknowledge and deal with our emotion healthily, it is likely to cause harm to us and others. It might get expressed through bouts of anger, physical problems, low-level depression or addictions. It is so important that we learn to understand our emotions and work through them well. So much of the internal freedom I now enjoy has been directly related to my increasing ability to identify and process my emotion in a healthy way. As leaders it is very difficult to lead people into freedom we haven't experienced ourselves. The more freedom we can get with our emotions the more effective we will be at helping others get free too.

The ideal destination we need to aim for is emotional health; feeling and expressing our emotions deeply but not being ruled by them. I was shut down emotionally for years, but over time as I have asked Jesus to connect my heart to His, my emotions have slowly come back to life. These days I am having to discover how to hold onto and believe the truth in the midst of feeling deeply. I still have a way to go in learning how to feel and express anger and experience fullness of joy, but I am moving in the right direction. In my experience, most leaders I meet and spend time with are more likely to have emotions that are shut down rather than being overly emotional. If that is your story, then be encouraged by mine; God can change your heart and breathe life back into what you feel. Can I urge you wholeheartedly not to settle for repressed emotions? Our desire as sons and daughters should be to become more and more like Jesus. He was and is the perfect example of emotional health and His longing for us is that we would be like Him.

The wonderful truth as we journey towards emotional health is that we are able to help those we are developing journey there too. The more we can equip people to be emotionally healthy, the more they will be able to step into freedom and be who God has called them to be. One of the key messages I teach is to do with how to process disappointment:[5] how to navigate mystery in the Kingdom so that you can stay in a place of faith and expectation. Whenever I teach this message it always comes with authority because I have lived the message personally so often; I have a lot of spiritual capital in this area. I could not tell you the number of people I have seen step into freedom as I have taught them how to process disappointment in a healthy way. So many believers are desperately trying to muster up faith to see God move only to find that disappointment is smothering their expectation. All people need is a bit of teaching and then a whole lot of permission and encouragement to feel and express their pain. Time and time again as people choose to open up their hearts to Jesus for healing, the result is renewed hope and reignited faith. The reason this is so exciting is that believers who are full of faith really believe that nothing is impossible for God.

How would you describe your emotional health? Are you someone who is in danger of becoming introspective because you are always searching your own heart? Do you often feel exhausted and overwhelmed by how much you feel all the time? Or are you someone who never looks below the surface because talking about emotions feels like trying to talk another language to you? Are you aware of your emotions simmering below the surface with no idea how to manage them? Whichever way you lean on the scale of emotional health, can I encourage you to invite the Holy Spirit to lead you towards the middle road; the road where you feel and express your emotions but they don't dominate you? It is in this place that sonship and daughterhood really flourishes.

## DO YOU KNOW YOUR PEOPLE?

Our TSM leadership team is made up of some of the most amazing people I know. In some ways we are really similar to each other and in other ways we are completely different. Learning to work together over the years has not always been straightforward, but it has been worth pushing through the awkward moments of misunderstanding to get to where we are today. We still have much to learn about each other, but more than ever our team feels like family; a family who trust each other, champion each other, value each other and have each other's backs. The great thing about being family as a team is that the people we lead quickly feel like family too. In the same way that what's inside us as individuals impacts those around us, how we relate together as a team shapes the things we lead. TSM feels like family because we feel like family as a team; mothers and fathers and brothers and sisters working together to see the students we are investing in succeed. Growing in self-awareness as an individual not only helps you to understand yourself better, it also makes you more likely to be mindful about wanting to understand your people.

Let me show you how this plays out with a couple of the TSM leadership team. Philbe is the only non-activator on a team of activators; people who love to make things happen as quickly as possible once decisions have been made. Historically, this has made Philbe feel lost in team meetings. She has had to battle lies that she is holding us back when she asks for more time to think about something the rest of us already agree on. I am sure some of the lies have stemmed from the frustration she has seen in some of our faces and heard in some of our responses. Being the 'odd one out' in this area could easily lead to Philbe holding back what she is thinking and feeling, and sadly at times this is exactly what has happened. Yet as we have sought to understand each other better, and as Philbe has been honest with us about how our fast-paced approach to things makes her feel, we have been able to adjust how we operate as a team. The truth is that when Philbe asks us to pause on a decision, it is for our best. Sometimes we have failed to think through all the implications of a decision for us or our students. Where rushing it through could have caused unnecessary damage, taking more time to think about it has often resulted in success. Philbe is such a gift to our team.

Jake is a very strategic thinker. He has a 'crow's nest' set of gifts where his mind is focused on the future. Jake's strengths are also a huge gift to our team, and they are so different to how I operate. I remember struggling to understand how he ticked when he first joined our team. I would regularly start meetings with a question about how we were doing personally before launching into all the business on the agenda. I am really passionate about building deep relationships with people so I want to be able to connect on a heart level. The rest of the team seemed to find it very straight-forward to know how they were doing and what was going on in their hearts. When it was Jake's turn to answer, it often felt that he struggled to know how to respond. I quickly interpreted Jake's faltering answers as an unwillingness to be authentic. That was until we had the StrengthsFinder[6] test we completed as a team analysed and explained by one of our elders.

Our elder encouraged us to picture Jake's mind as a house. Where the rest of us spend a lot of our time hanging out in the lounge, finding it very comfortable to connect and relate to each other, Jake is in an entirely different room. The way Jake's brain is wired means that he spends a lot of his time in the attic, thinking about and looking towards the future. When he is asked a question that requires him to join us in the lounge and look into his heart, it takes time. Figuratively speaking, he has to come out of the attic, walk down the stairs and into the lounge in order to connect with the question being asked. Jake's somewhat faltering answers were not an unwillingness to be authentic, they were simply down to the fact that he was having to do a long walk in his brain in order to work out what he was feeling. The transition from focusing on the future to looking into your heart is not a quick one.

As we have taken time to understand more about how Jake ticks, we have been able to adjust how we operate as a team. We tend not to ask Jake heart questions first so that he has time to leave the attic before he has to answer, although to his credit, the walk to the lounge is getting quicker and quicker. I am so glad I understand Jake better than I used to, and I am so glad he spends a chunk of his time in the attic. I think if all of us were in the lounge we would miss some of what God wants to lead us into as a school. I have real value and respect for what Jake carries and how he is wired.

I am nervous about oversimplifying the complexities of working in team. I have just unpacked a snapshot of the strengths and gifts that Philbe and Jake carry. I could have done the same with Marco and Rah and myself. We are multifaceted people with different strengths and weaknesses, passions and insecurities, hopes and fears. Some of our strengths overlap, some of our strengths mean we approach situations from completely different perspectives. None of us can be neatly defined by labels or put into boxes; we definitely colour outside the lines and we still have to work hard at understanding each other. In a nutshell that sums up the point I want to make.

If I want to be a leader who sees those I am championing succeed in God, I need to work really hard at knowing the people I have around me. This calls for security in my daughterhood because it requires me to admit that I am not the whole answer and my way is not the only way to do something. I need to steer clear of judging those who are different to me. As leaders we need to make it our aim, with great patience and grace, to understand how people tick so we can celebrate who they are and draw the best out of them. When we grow in self-awareness as leaders, we are more likely to be mindful about wanting to understand those we lead. The more we understand the people we invest in, the more we can see them succeed.

Do you know who you are?

Do you know your strengths and the things you need to grow in to minimise your weaknesses?

Would you describe yourself as being emotionally healthy?

Do you know how the people you lead are different to you and how you can draw the best out of them?

Before you start beating yourself up, all of these questions need to be answered against the backdrop of God's delight and pleasure over you. You need to hear His 'well done' ringing loudly in your ears. The truth is that none of us can answer these questions with a resounding 'yes'. There is always more for us to discover about ourselves and always more for us to learn as we develop others. The point of the questions is to prompt us to go on a journey of self-discovery with the Holy Spirit, where He highlights when we need to change and we willingly follow His lead. Our journey into sonship and daughterhood must be initiated and directed by the Holy Spirit; our responsibility is to keep saying yes to Him.

Recently, when I was spending time with God, I had a major revelation that is changing how I see myself and how I approach my journey into daughterhood. I was reflecting on my day, thinking through where I had acted like an orphan and the aspects of my character I wanted to change. As I was focused on my weaknesses and the things I lacked, God cut across my thoughts with His perspective. He told me that when He looks at me and reflects on my day He focuses only on the gold. I realised in that moment that God is not looking at who I'm not or where I lack, rather He is celebrating and calling out of me who I am. This was a jaw-dropping encounter as I caught a glimpse of the stark difference between the way God viewed me and the way I saw myself. I am now on a journey of trying to be more mindful of the gold that God sees. I want to move away from pursuing revelation of my daughterhood from a place of knowing my lack and brokenness, which easily leads to performance and trying really hard to change. Instead I want to grow in my identity from a place of faith and freedom, being mindful of the great qualities God has put in me and using these as a launch pad into more. If God focuses on the gold in me, then He does the same with you. How are you doing at seeing what He sees?

# 3. CULTURE FACILITATES GROWTH

Writing this chapter has been a real challenge because words on a page feel so inadequate in describing something like culture that really needs to be experienced and caught. It is very difficult to appreciate how much of an impact culture can have until you are in it and encountering it first-hand. Culture is not theoretical, it is tangible. Having walked through our culture journey as a church, and seen the impact it has had on us corporately and in my own life, I am a huge culture advocate. I have also had the privilege of seeing the influence of our culture on hundreds of TSM students over the years. The culture we create at TSM is one of my favourite things about the school.

Many students come to TSM not really knowing who they are and carrying heaviness and pain. They leave us after nine months with greater security in their identity and a new-found confidence to embrace the unique calling on their lives. Some students actually look physically different at the end of TSM because of what God does in them. I am convinced that one of the key reasons we see our students experience freedom and feel empowered to step into what God has for them is our culture. We are intentional at TSM about creating a culture that makes people feel valued and safe, where people can be fully themselves without fear of judgement or rejection. We aim to establish an environment where people are championed and believed in, and where they are encouraged to live lives of radical obedience to God. We have found that an intentionally defined culture facilitates growth.

The journey of one particular student stands out in my mind. A lovely lady in her late fifties attended the school a few years ago. It was clear very quickly that she was struggling with life. She would sit through worship and teaching sessions with her arms folded and often with an intense frown on her face. It was obvious through interactions with her that she was carrying a lot of pain. She was disappointed that God seemed to be meeting with everyone else but her and she was envious of other students' breakthroughs. At times she would tell us in no uncertain terms that she did not want to be at the school and on the odd occasion she would refuse to join in with what we were asking the students to do. It would have been easy to withdraw from this student because she was prickly and, at times, challenging. Instead, our team kept pursuing her, accepting her where she was at and loving her. Bit by bit her walls started to come down.

On one occasion our student got angry with one of the TSM team because of something he was asking her to do. Instead of rejecting or rebuking the student, our team member thanked her for being brave in sharing her heart and encouraged her to keep being authentic about what she was feeling. The continued acceptance this student received helped her to feel safe to tentatively take her mask off and show us who she really was. It turned out that this amazing lady, although she had been a Christian for more than thirty years, had doubts about whether

God really existed. She struggled to encounter His love and would say that He never spoke to her. Our culture enabled this student to stop pretending and instead be honest for the first time about her doubts and fears. As she brought the pain and anger in her heart into the light, God was able to break in and bring incredible freedom.

This courageous lady changed so much throughout her TSM journey. By the end of the year much of the pain she had been carrying was gone, and as a result she was so much softer and she knew much more joy. She started to engage in worship and she learned that God did speak to her. As she embraced her new-found freedom she began to bring words of knowledge and pray for people at her home church, and she also joined us on a ministry trip to Scotland to impart some of the freedom she had found to others. This precious student's heart was brought back to life by God's love. I believe our culture was instrumental in enabling her to access and then encounter God's kindness, which then resulted in her experiencing breakthrough. A Kingdom culture is the springboard for people's freedom and it fast-tracks their development and growth.

## DEFINING CULTURE

Creating culture within a group of people is a little like a farmer nurturing a crop. Now admittedly I'm no farmer, but I do understand the importance of cultivating the ground to give crops the best possible chance for success. If soil is too hard or if it is full of weeds, crops will struggle to flourish. Farmers take time to till the ground in order to prepare the soil and remove anything that might hinder growth. They also intentionally add in substances like compost to create an environment that maximises a crop's chance of development. The better the environment seeds are sown into, the greater the likelihood of a good crop. The success of a crop is directly related to the kind of culture the farmer creates for it.

The kind of culture we create as leaders is just as significant when it comes to seeing those we lead grow and bear fruit. As with the farming analogy, there are certain environments that will stunt an individual's growth. If, for example, we have a culture of mockery where we tear one another down with our words or we are quick to belittle people when they make mistakes, those we are leading are unlikely to feel safe to be themselves or to take risks. If people do not feel free to be themselves or to take risks, then they cannot grow. On the other hand, if the culture we create focuses on encouraging people in their uniqueness and championing them when they take risks in obedience to God irrespective of the outcome, the people we are developing are much more likely to flourish in God. The success of the people we lead is directly related to the culture we create for them.

We went on a journey at King's Arms more than ten years ago of intentionally defining our culture. We had defined our vision; what we felt called to and where we were going as a church. We regularly set year-long goals to define our next steps in fulfilling that vision. What we had not done was define our culture; decide the kind of people we wanted to be on the way to realising our calling. We learned fairly quickly that every organisation has a culture, whether it is intentionally established or not. We could either let our culture come about by accident and risk leaving weeds in the soil that would hinder our growth, or we could be intentional about creating a culture that enabled people to thrive. We decided to go on a journey of working out the kind of people we wanted to be as we went about the work God had called us to do.

Defining a culture in your church, your workplace or in your family is not something that happens overnight. It is not about choosing random words to define who you want to be, writing them on a piece of paper and then pinning them on a wall for everyone to see. Establishing a culture takes time, discussion and repetition. People need to own it, leaders need to model it and you need to be intentional about walking it out. It took us several months as a church to choose the words we wanted to use to define who we wanted to be. There were multiple discussions among the elders, senior leaders and small-group leaders before the final five words were chosen. Then we had to take time to unpack the words and work out what they actually looked like in practice so that we could communicate them clearly. Establishing culture is not about memorising a few key words, it is about changing the way we think about God, ourselves and others so that we actually live differently.

I honestly think the culture we are trying to create as a church and at TSM is one of the main reasons for the fruit we enjoy as a family. It is certainly the reason why so many in our community feel empowered to step into the things God has called them to. When you intentionally create a culture that believes the best about people, that celebrates each other's strengths while covering their weaknesses, and that encourages people to take risks with God, you create an environment where people cannot help but grow. Of course, we do not demonstrate our culture perfectly; there are still a lot of areas for us to mature in, both individually and corporately, and there is still much for us to learn. Yet the great thing about having our culture defined is that we have something to aim for and work towards. Bit by bit we are seeing people change and we are enjoying good fruit.

## CULTURE FLOWS FROM THE INSIDE OUT

The culture in a church, workplace or family is decided on and modelled by its leaders. This is a real privilege, but it also comes with sobering responsibility. It is very difficult to influence a culture if the culture we want to create does not first exist in our own heart. The reality is that the culture within us as leaders is the culture that will flow out of us through our leadership; whatever is going on inside of us is what will come out of us. This means it is not enough to simply communicate the cultural behaviours we want those we lead to embrace, we have to internalise and live out those cultural values ourselves. This can take real humility and focused time with Jesus to change the way we think and to enable us to experience greater internal freedom. Modelling culture as leaders is not about working really hard to modify our behaviour. Rather, it is about inviting Jesus to work on our hearts so that we become the culture.

One of our cultural values at TSM is authenticity. I unpack its importance in more detail in the next chapter, but essentially it is about showing people who you really are rather than hiding behind a mask. I remember sharing with our students, before I gave a talk, about some anxiety I was wrestling with. It was not chronic anxiety that many sadly suffer with, yet I had never experienced this kind of anxiety before and the symptoms were scary and stifling. I was often on the verge of tears for what seemed like no apparent reason and everything in me wanted to run and hide. As I chose to be authentic with the students, I encouraged anyone who could relate to what I had been feeling to stand. I really felt like God wanted to bring encouragement and freedom to those in the same boat as me. I was shocked as approximately thirty students stood to their feet around the room. My choice to share vulnerably gave others permission to be authentic too. We had a great time of praying for each other and calling on God for anxiety to be replaced by His peace.

There is a big difference between teaching the theory of a culture and modelling it in reality. I could have shared someone else's experience of anxiety and reinforced the rationale behind why choosing to be authentic is a good thing, but it would not have carried as much weight. There is a big emphasis in the church today on intellectual capital; what information do you have that you can impart to me? Many people get their significance and value from the amount of information they retain that they can then pass on to others. Personally, I am increasingly eager to cultivate spiritual capital: the ability to impart not just information but personal revelation. Spiritual capital is seen when leaders share from their own personal experience: situations they are walking through with God, battles they have won by using Scripture, breakthrough they are seeing as they pray. When a leader speaks with spiritual capital it is not just theory, they have lived what they talk about, which means what they say really packs a punch.

Of course, no one can demonstrate culture perfectly; we are all on a journey. The key for us as leaders as we look to define our culture is that we invite people to journey with us. Our ultimate aim in intentionally defining culture is not that we teach people a set of external behaviours to follow. Our aim is to see people transformed in their hearts and thinking so that cultural behaviours become the natural outworking of internal change. This will only happen if we first pursue change in our own lives. What does the culture in your own heart look like? Are you more secure in your identity today than you were last year? Are you feeling more empowered to do what God has called you to, or have you shrunk back? The more freedom you have personally, the more you will be able to lead others into freedom. Your internal culture will impact the culture you create around you.

## UNPACKING CULTURE

Once culture is defined it then needs to be unpacked so that people understand what it actually looks like in practice. As a church we decided on five key words to define the culture we want to build and we have the same culture at TSM. Over the years of seeing our culture in action, I have experienced its impact personally in a number of different ways. It has changed how I relate to God and how I think about myself. It has also influenced the way that I lead and, as a result, the impact of my leadership on those I invest in. The cultural words we chose do not encompass everything we want to be on our journey of following Jesus, but they are a great foundation. Each culture word, once unpacked, helps to create an environment that facilitates growth in every person who chooses to embrace it.

The five culture words we decided on as a church were honour, authenticity, acceptance, generosity and courage. I will briefly unpack each cultural value below. The written word cannot do culture justice, it really needs to be experienced. What follows will at least give you a flavour of what our culture looks like when it is lived out.

## Honour

Honour means to recognise a person's true value and worth and to treat them accordingly. Scripture instructs us to honour God, 'You are worthy, our Lord and God, to receive glory and honour and power...' (Revelation 4:11). It encourages us to honour ourselves; to recognise our own inherent value because we have been made in the image and likeness of God: 'I praise you because I am fearfully and wonderfully made; your works are wonderful, I know that full well' (Psalm 139:14). It also teaches us to honour others because they have value and worth too. Peter sums up the call to honour others brilliantly when he writes in his letter, 'Honour everyone...' (1 Peter 2:17, ESV). In a world where dishonour is rife, where 'God' is a curse word and people tear themselves and others down, a culture of honour really stands out. I think that is the reason it has such an impact on people when they experience it and embrace it.

Honouring God is essential if people want to grow and step into all they are called to. When we live our lives with God at the centre, we make what He wants for us more important than anything else. The truth is that what God wants for our lives is the very best for us. Honouring God also enables us to accomplish far more than we ever could in our own strength because it causes us to depend on Him. When we are dependent on God, anything is possible for us. As leaders it must be our priority to point those we lead to Jesus; to help them fall more in love with Him so that He remains at the centre of their lives. When those we are developing honour God above everything else, they will grow in their sonship and daughterhood and, as a result, have greater impact on the world around them.

It is also important that we help those we are investing in to honour themselves. So many believers I meet struggle to fully embrace the influence they are called to have because they doubt their value and worth. They limit their gifts and downplay their strengths because they spend so much time comparing themselves to others rather than celebrating who God has made them to be. In my experience, speaking truth to people and encouraging them has had a very significant impact on those I lead. If you can help someone to believe that what God says about them is actually true, and that the extent of His love for them was demonstrated at the cross, it has the potential to change everything. In a culture of honour, people learn to see themselves as God sees them. When people understand their inherent value and worth, they stop hiding and instead start to thrive.

I remember a guy in his fifties getting major breakthrough on TSM as he started to see himself as God saw him. This amazing man was wracked with guilt and shame because of a divorce earlier in his life, which left him estranged from his children. The shame he felt caused him to isolate himself from the rest of the students and he would often sit on his own at the back of the room. This man was hugely gifted, he was gentle and safe and called to be a father to many, yet the negative opinion he had of himself stopped him believing it. My friend's breakthrough came one afternoon as some of the students and I prayed for him.

We started to speak truth over this father. His head was bowed and he was clearly struggling to receive what was being prayed. I cannot remember exactly what I said, but in essence I encouraged this student to lift his head and to look up. I told him that he did not have to live in shame any more because he was a dearly loved son of God. As my friend tentatively lifted his head, something supernatural happened as tears started to roll down his face. It was as if something shifted in his heart and he was able to embrace the truth about his value and worth in a new way. As a result of this encounter, the whole countenance of our student changed; love started to radiate from his face. In the weeks that followed he started to connect with other students, he shared stories from the front with confidence and he increasingly stepped into the fathering role God always intended Him to have. My friend learned how to live as a son rather than an orphan.

Teaching people to honour themselves is a huge key in seeing them accomplish everything God has called them to. It is also really important in the process of equipping them to honour others. The more you understand and experience the extent to which God honours you, the more you are able to see others through the same lens. When we honour others, we learn to celebrate the ways they are different to us, we are able to disagree with people but still maintain unity, and we treat people based on their identity in Christ rather than their background or behaviour. When we honour everyone as leaders we create a spacious place for people to flourish. When we teach those we lead to do the same, that spacious place grows and expands as more and more people feel believed in and empowered to impact the world around them. Why not make it your aim in your church, workplace and family to 'outdo one another in showing honour'? (Romans 12:10, ESV).

## Authenticity and Acceptance

Authenticity and acceptance go hand in hand. It is very difficult to create a culture of authenticity if you do not also have a culture of acceptance. Authenticity at its core means to show people who you really are. It involves being honest about your struggles as well as being upfront about your gifts and calling. It requires people to come out of hiding and be seen. Acceptance provides the safe place that authenticity needs to thrive. People are unlikely to step fully into the light if they are afraid of being ridiculed, misunderstood or judged. A culture of acceptance prioritises demonstrating kindness, patience and forgiveness to everyone. When we accept and love people for who they really are, we give them permission to fall apart as well as permission to succeed.

I remember when a TSM student approached me with a nervous look on her face saying she needed to confess something. When students apply to do TSM they fill in an application form so that we can learn about who they are and what makes them tick. Some of the questions ask about a student's past and their family so that we can understand people's backgrounds as well as their current situation. This particular student had lied on her application form. She had chosen to hide the fact that her husband was a member of the Freemasons because she was afraid and ashamed. Two months before school ended she felt convicted to come and tell me the truth.

In the past I might have got angry with this student for hiding the truth and I'm sure I would have judged her for her lack of integrity. Yet my daughterhood meant it never even crossed my mind to respond in these ways. A harsh response would have reinforced the shame my friend already felt and taught her that authenticity was too risky; that in the future she should just keep things hidden. What actually flowed out of my heart was encouragement for this courageous student for being vulnerable and bringing what was hidden into the light. I demonstrated acceptance and responded with love and grace. Accepting this student did not mean that I ignored her lie or that I neglected to challenge her. In a culture of authenticity things confessed sometimes carry consequences and require correction. Acceptance does not mean that 'anything goes' and that we do not challenge people when we need to. What it does mean is that we believe the best about people and when we do challenge, we do it with genuine love in our heart.

Personally, being in a culture of authenticity and acceptance has been the main catalyst for me stepping into my identity as a daughter of God. I came to King's Arms with lots of pain and disappointment. I did not know who I was and I wrestled with lots of lies, fears and insecurities. I have been encouraged to be authentic over the years and my authenticity has been consistently met with acceptance and love. As a result, bit by bit my walls have come down; pain has been processed, lies have been exposed and I have increasingly encountered God's love. I hate to think where or who I would be today if I had kept everything hidden inside me rather than feeling safe to bring it into the light. A culture of authenticity and acceptance is crucial for us as leaders and those we are championing to access the freedom Jesus won for us on the cross. How are you doing at showing people who you really are? Do you demonstrate love and acceptance when people make themselves vulnerable with you? These cultural values make it so much easier for us to stop living as orphans and instead embrace our sonship and daughterhood.

## Generosity

We follow a lavishly generous Father. In His generosity He sent Jesus to die in our place. Jesus, in His desire to see us enjoy life in abundance, made Himself nothing and took on the nature of a servant. He gave up everything so that we could inherit everything and He took great joy in doing it. In a culture of generosity, people are encouraged to sacrifice and serve out of the overflow of what the Father has done for them. Leaders in this kind of culture lay their lives down to promote and empower others, rather than focus on establishing their own ministry or reputation. One of my favourite things about leading is seeing the people around me grow in God; there is so much joy to be had in witnessing the success of those you lead. In a culture of generosity, people are served and celebrated and championed. They also get to glimpse more of God's love for them and His desire to provide for them out of His unlimited resources.

One Saturday during a TSM outreach afternoon on the streets of Bedford, one of our students had her bike stolen. This particular student was doing TSM for a second time. She is one of the most courageous people I know and had pushed through so much fear to attend the school. The student was totally dependent on her bike as her primary mode of transport and she did not earn enough money to be able to replace it. It was such a discouragement to her when she realised it was gone. Once outreach had finished and we headed back to the church, some of the team floated the idea of taking up a spontaneous offering for this student, to go towards replacing her bike. This is the way you begin to think when you are in a culture of generosity.

The team announced to the rest of the students what had happened to their peer's bike and then shared their idea to take up an offering. One by one different students opened their purses and wallets to offer money in support of this lady. By the time the money had been gathered together and counted we had raised over £300, which was more than enough for our student to get a new bike. This lavish gift of money overwhelmed our student so much that she had to leave the room. In that moment she got a greater glimpse, not only of God's love for her, but also His desire to abundantly meet her needs. She also got a greater revelation of her value in the TSM family, as friends and strangers alike sacrificed financially on her behalf. It was a beautiful moment.

When we create a culture of generosity we replicate in a small way what God is like. We remember that He is a lavish Father who wants to bless His children. We remind ourselves that He has all the resources we need to accomplish all He has called us to do. In a culture of generosity, people are empowered to embrace their unique gifts and abilities. They are also inspired to lay their lives down for people around them because they understand that others' success is their success. Being generous means to live with a king's heart and a servant's hands. In other words, our ability to create this kind of culture is directly related to our awareness of our identity as dearly loved sons and daughters of the King. The more we understand who we are, the more we are free to lay our lives down for the people around us. How are you doing at receiving God's generosity towards you so that you can give it away to others?

## Courage

A culture of courage says: 'He is a big God, have a go.' God loves to call us to things that are beyond our natural capabilities so that we have to depend on Him and He gets all the glory. In order to access the unique calling on our lives we have to take risks; we have to step out of our comfort zone and give things a go. Often the way we learn and grow is by making mistakes and getting things wrong. If we create a culture where mistakes are not OK and where caution is championed over risk, people around us are likely to settle and stagnate. However, when we encourage risk-taking and we celebrate courage we release those we are developing to grow in their gifts. In a culture of courage, people often realise they are able to achieve so much more than they thought, because with God anything is possible.

One of our TSM students who works for an asset management company in London felt God give her a dream about running an

Alpha course[7] for her colleagues. She quickly shelved the dream because she lacked confidence and felt she would never get the permission she needed. As she stepped into the culture of courage at TSM and she started to understand more of who God said she was as His daughter, her thinking started to change. This student began to realise that her responsibility was to be obedient to God and that He was then in charge of the outcome of her obedience. The pressure was not on her to make something happen. All she needed to do was muster up ten seconds of courage to seek permission from her boss and the rest was then up to God.

This courageous student bit the bullet and asked the question of her boss as part of a review meeting she was in. His immediate response of 'yes' took her somewhat by surprise and before she knew it she was leading her first-ever Alpha course in her workplace. Throughout the duration of the course, twelve of her colleagues dipped in and out of the lunchtime sessions. Our student engaged in multiple conversations about faith and what she believed, and she even took the opportunity to pray for certain colleagues for healing. Amidst misunderstanding and mockery, this amazing lady leaned into God and He carried her through, teaching her that with Him she was capable of much more than she realised. At TSM this student entered into a culture that said, 'Why not you?' She stepped into a culture that champions courage. The result was that she grew in her gifts and abilities as she increasingly embraced God's unique call over her life.

Courage looks different for different people. For some, courage looks like talking to a stranger, bringing a prophetic word or standing up for what you believe in your workplace. For others, it takes courage to have an honest conversation, to go through the process of buying a house on your own or to share the dreams God has put in your heart. Whatever courage looks like for us and the people we lead, the key is that we create a culture that champions people's choice to step out of their comfort zone and lean into Jesus. The truth is that whenever we make the choice to be courageous, irrespective of the outcome, we always grow. How are you doing at modelling being courageous as a leader? The extent to which we model courage in our own lives is the extent to which those we are championing will feel permission to do the same.

The five cultural values I have unpacked summarise the culture we are going after as a church and at TSM.[8] We do not live this culture perfectly, but we have definitely seen significant fruit by intentionally defining the kind of people we want to be as we pursue our vision. As you embrace the culture journey, please resist the temptation to simply adopt the same words for your own area of influence. As I have already said, defining the culture you want to create takes time. It requires discussion and reflection and careful consideration of the kind of people God is uniquely calling you to be. It also requires an honest look at the culture you are currently part of in order to identify what needs to change so that God's Kingdom can break in. Defining a culture that facilitates growth does not happen overnight but it is easily worth the effort when you see the fruit it produces in the people who embrace it.

Culture is key when it comes to creating a spacious place for the people we lead to flourish. It is possible to intentionally create an environment that removes barriers and blockages to people's growth and instead facilitates and multiplies fruit. The most important thing for us as leaders is being mindful of the culture in our own hearts. It is very difficult to teach people to honour themselves if we do not like who God has made us to be. Equally, the permission people need to embrace a culture of authenticity will come from our choices to be authentic. The same principle applies for the cultural values you choose to adopt. Whatever is going on inside us is what will come out of us to shape the culture around us. This is why growing in our sonship and daughterhood and leading out of this identity is so vital.

What kind of culture are you creating through your leadership?
Are the people you're developing growing in God and bearing fruit?
Are you prioritising your own relationship with God so that your leadership flows out of your sonship or daughterhood?

Our main priority as leaders must be our own relationship with God, where we learn how to live as His dearly loved children. The more we understand who God says we are, the less our old orphan thinking has room to influence our behaviour. Sons and daughters know what their Father is like. They understand His heart, the way He thinks and feels about people and His desire to champion His kids and see them succeed. The more we lead out of our sonship or daughterhood, the more we are able to represent the Father to the people around us. Not only that, we are also able to represent the culture of His Kingdom. A culture of freedom and life, where expectation is high and joy abounds. When the people we are leading step into this kind of culture, anything is possible.

## 4. LEAD WITHOUT A MASK

My journey out of orphan thinking and into daughterhood started years ago. God has been so kind to gently and consistently put His finger on pain in my heart and lies in my head that stop me living out of my true identity. Over the years, as I have spent time with God and encountered His love in worship and through His Word, and as I have asked friends to pray with me, I have been able to step into so much freedom. Some of the fruit of the journey I have been on is that I am now comfortable in my own skin, I am increasingly confident in who I am called to be and I know that my Father is for me and that He has my back. Much of the freedom I now enjoy and the legacy of freedom we are building as a church family can be traced back to one pivotal Sunday morning when Simon, our lead elder, chose to lead without a mask. Simon made a decision to let approximately two hundred of us see his very personal and vulnerable journey. His authenticity acted as a launch pad for many of us to access the freedom God had for us too.

I had been leading for a few years by this point, and although the areas I was leading were generally going well, I had been feeling for a while that I needed some internal freedom. Something on the inside of me did not feel right. I wrestled with a constant unsettledness in my heart, which made it difficult for me to access God's peace. As a result, I often felt driven in my leadership and I was regularly uptight and intense because I was desperate to please the people around me. My hunch was that I needed some deliverance; that I needed to be set free from some spiritual oppression, but I felt bad about having these thoughts. I genuinely believed that as a leader I should not need to be set free. I believed the lie that to be a good leader I should always have it together and show no signs of weakness. Praise God that this particular Sunday morning Simon modelled to me that leaders need freedom too.

I will never forget the honesty with which Simon shared as he told us about his time in Oklahoma, USA. He had received prayer ministry from a lady named Diane and then a man called Brother Nelson. Brother Nelson was known as the 'deliverance guy' and Diane had referred Simon to him for a second day of prayer; she thought that he needed some freedom. After talking with Simon for a while, Brother Nelson stopped mid-sentence to ask Simon if he had ever repented of the sin of pride; not the pride of arrogance or haughtiness, but the pride of self-reliance. As Simon relayed the story, he told us that in that moment God took him through major deliverance on Diane's sofa, setting him free from a spiritual stronghold of self-reliance. It was evident that something really significant had happened to Simon as he shared with us from his heart.

I remember feeling a mix of emotions as Simon told us the journey he had been on. I felt incredible gratitude for the courage he demonstrated in choosing to be authentic with us as a church family. I felt immediately more connected to him and a deeper sense of respect for him. My overriding emotion was one of relief. Simon's story gave me the permission I needed to seek God for my own internal freedom. At the end of the service, Simon invited people in the room to stand if they felt like they needed some breakthrough. I was one of many to respond, and all around the room people began to encounter God's love and get set free. Very quickly after I stood up, I was delivered from spiritual oppression connected to the fear of death. The internal angst I had been feeling was finally gone, and it had gone as a result of Simon's decision to lead without a mask.

I found out years later that Simon and Paul, who were leading the church together at the time, had discussed at length whether or not Simon should share what had happened to him in the States with the rest of the church. I am so glad they decided to go for it. Allowing people to see your journey as a leader, to see who you really are, is risky. You cannot control how people will respond or what they will do with the information they have. Yet, thought through wisely, the potential benefits of authenticity far outweigh the possible costs. We would not be where we are now as a church if Simon had not chosen to let us in on his journey into freedom. Leading without a mask is crucial if we want to empower those we lead to be everything God has called them to be.

## AUTHENTICITY UNVEILED

Authenticity at its core is about being real and genuine. It is about removing façades so that people can see who you really are; both your struggles and your successes. If you are not secure in your identity as a son or daughter of God, you will prefer to keep your mask on as you lead because you are likely to feel more comfortable when there is distance between you and the people around you. If you lead with an orphan heart, your identity will be wrapped up in what people think about you rather than what the Father says about you. This makes it especially risky for you to show any signs of weakness or areas of struggle. You will probably have thoughts like, 'if people really knew me, they wouldn't want to follow me' and so you feel safer with your mask firmly in place. Leading as an orphan will also mean you shy away from showing people your strengths or celebrating your breakthroughs through fear of coming across as being proud.

When you understand how loved you are by God and that His love for you is nothing to do with your performance but all because of His amazing grace, you can lead out of a place of security; you can lead without a mask. You can be transparent with those you are developing about your weaknesses and struggles because you know that these things do not define who you are in Christ. When you lead as a son or daughter, you have confidence that the more people see who you really are the more likely they are to be inspired to follow you, not the other way around. Even if people do respond to your authenticity with criticism it no longer rocks you because your focus is on what your Heavenly Father says about you rather than what people think. You will also find it easier to be honest about your strengths and to celebrate your successes because you understand that when you do it gives glory to God.

Jesus really championed authenticity through His leadership. He seemed to be drawn to the weak and the broken, to people who were not pretending they had it all together and who did not hide who they really were. In contrast He was in regular confrontation with the Pharisees, the religious leaders of the day, whose primary focus was on managing their outward appearance. The Pharisees prioritised their own and others' external behaviour over and above the condition of their heart. By leading with their masks firmly in place, the Pharisees were able to 'keep up appearances' in public and create a dividing wall between themselves and anyone they considered 'less religious'. The problem with this kind of leadership is that Jesus is not interested in religion and He is not a fan of behaviour management or pretending. Jesus is looking for the real deal; He is after our hearts.

When our masks come off, Jesus can really begin to work with us and empower us in His Kingdom. We see this in action when Jesus reinstates Peter to his position of leadership in the church after His resurrection. When Jesus is led away to be crucified, Peter makes the biggest mistake of his life. He denies any knowledge of or history with Jesus; he abandons Jesus in His time of greatest need. No doubt Peter would have thought he had blown the promises Jesus had spoken over his life. My hunch is that Jesus actually saw Peter's moment of weakness as a launch pad into them. All of a sudden, Peter's bravado was gone and his vulnerability was on show for all to see; his mask was well and truly off. Peter interpreted his vulnerability as weakness, as something that disqualified him. I wonder if Jesus interpreted it as an opportunity for Peter to learn greater dependence on his Heavenly Father for all he was called to in the future.

As well as being drawn to authenticity, I love the way Jesus modelled it by showing people who He was and what was going on in His heart. Jesus was not reluctant to show His emotions. He openly expressed anger when He drove money changers out of the Temple with a whip of cords (John 2:13-16), He was 'full of joy through the Holy Spirit' (Luke 10:21), He was deeply moved and wept unashamedly at Lazarus' tomb even though He was about to raise him from the dead (John 11), and He allowed His disciples to see His profound sorrow at the thought of going to the cross (Matthew 26:36-38). Jesus championed authenticity and He modelled it, which in turn enabled the disciples to really connect with Him as they learned from Him. The disciples did not have to learn from a distance. Jesus invited them to journey alongside Him; He welcomed them to do life with Him.

When you lead without a mask, you create a safe place for the people around you to be all God has called them to be. I am sure there are many more benefits to authenticity than those I outline below, but these are some my favourite reasons to fight to keep my mask off as I invest in others.

## GATEWAY TO PERSONAL FREEDOM

Authenticity enables us to access the freedom Jesus won for us on the cross. John 10:10 tells us that Jesus came so that we could know life in all its fullness. This scripture is not meant to be relegated to an inspirational quote we know in our heads but do not really believe in our hearts: it is actually true. Jesus' death and resurrection makes it possible for us to be fully alive on the inside. 'I will give you a new heart and put a new spirit in you; I will remove from you your heart of stone and give you a heart of flesh'

(Ezekiel 36:26). It is our inheritance as God's children to know freedom from sin and shame and pain and lies, which hold us back, and to receive God's forgiveness and love and freedom and truth, which propel us forward.

The enemy wants us to stay trapped as orphans, listening to his lies above the truth about our identity in Christ, but God has called us to be free sons and daughters. The way we access and live in the good of who God says we are is through authenticity. When we admit the lies we believe out loud, we break the power they have in our lives. This then creates space for the truth to take root in our hearts and our thinking. When we confess our struggles with sin to God and to trusted friends, shame is broken and we are able to receive and enjoy God's forgiveness. When we are real about and express our pain and disappointment, we are able to keep our hearts soft and open to God and to others. Authenticity is the gateway to personal freedom, and that freedom enables us to access life in abundance.

Authenticity is not only the gateway to our own personal freedom. When we take our masks off as leaders and model authenticity to those we lead, it increases the likelihood that they will access the freedom Jesus won for them too. Our honesty gives those around us permission to take their masks off and creates a safe place for them to deal with the things that hold them back. One of my favourite things about leading without a mask is seeing believers all around me encounter the freedom Jesus won for them as they take their masks off too.

Of course, when a leader chooses to model authenticity it is important that we are wise when deciding what to share and with whom. If we share too much it could have a negative effect on those we are developing, burdening them unnecessarily and creating an atmosphere of fear rather than faith and safety. Leading without a mask does not mean that we are always an open book; confessing everything to everyone. As leaders we need our safe people just as much as anyone else; those who know everything about us and still love us. What is important is that we do not use the need to be wise as an excuse for being guarded and keeping things hidden. I think many of us as leaders are not in danger of saying too much. Rather, we need to fight the very real trap of saying nothing at all.

## I CAN DO THAT!

Authenticity also helps to break down some of the barriers that can exist between those who lead and those who are being led. The sad thing about leaders who look as if they have everything together is that it makes it difficult for anyone to aspire to be like them. People who are acutely aware of their own weaknesses quickly discount themselves from the call of God on their lives because it has not been modelled to them that it is OK to be weak. Conversely, when we show people who we really are and we are honest about our vulnerabilities, we all start from a level playing field; we all get to go on a journey together, equally empowered to be everything God has called us to be.

I remember seeing this first-hand at our TSM launch weekend one year. We start our TSM school with a Friday evening and Saturday day event. The idea behind this time together is to give students and team the opportunity to connect with each other over an extended period. The weekend also helps to immerse the students in our school culture, which in turn fast-tracks them on their TSM journey. There is often a lot of fear in the room as the students gather for the first time. They know that TSM is likely to have a significant impact on their walk with God, but they have no idea what the journey is going to look like. Lots of new people in a room with lots of unknowns can easily lead to heightened anxiety. We purposely start the Friday evening with a light-hearted 'getting to know you' activity to help people relax. After the fun activity we share the vision of the school.

On this particular occasion Marco, who leads the evening school, got up to share the vision of TSM, exhorting the students to embrace a lifestyle of courage during their time with us. As part of his talk he shared very honestly about the fear he had wrestled with that week while he was preparing what to say. He told the students how he had talked about his fear with the rest of the team so that they could encourage him and speak truth to him. It was evident to everyone that we were watching a lifestyle of courage in action as Marco spoke that evening. Marco's choice to model authenticity to the students and to share his own struggle with fear resulted in a complete change of atmosphere in the room. You could literally feel fear dissipating and faith rising in its place. It was as if the students went from thinking, 'I don't think I can do this' to 'well, if he can do it, maybe I can too'. Marco's honesty dealt with any perceived hierarchy there could have been between students and team; suddenly we were all embarking on the TSM journey together.

## PERMISSION TO FLOURISH

Leading without a mask is not just about showing those you lead your personal challenges and areas of weakness, it also involves being honest about your strengths and the things God has called you to. If we want those we invest in to flourish in their walk with God, we have to model that flourishing is actually OK.

Under the guise of humility leaders can often shy away from talking about the things they are good at, the gifts God has given them, or the prophetic promises they are living with. The wrong belief behind this orphan behaviour is that talking about yourself positively is rooted in pride and results in self-promotion. The fear is that if we speak well of ourselves we will come across as arrogant or somehow take glory away from God. As a result we become experts at using self-deprecation in an attempt to keep ourselves humble, or at least keep the appearance of humility. The tragedy about this kind of leadership is that we inadvertently teach those we lead that it is not godly for them to be significant or successful.

In contrast, sons and daughters realise that their Heavenly Father is excited about celebrating who they are. They understand that talking honestly about their gifts and successes actually brings glory to God rather than taking it from Him. Every prophetic promise fulfilled in our lives and every breakthrough we get to be part of is all because of God's grace: it all points to Him. It does not honour the giver of the gift when we undermine the gift, and it does not honour the artist when we criticise the piece of art. God has lovingly crafted us with all of our unique skills and talents. As leaders it is crucial that we fully and joyfully embrace who God has made us to be. When we celebrate who we are and choose not to shy away from who God has called us to be, we give permission to those we have influence over to do the same.

As we give people permission to succeed, it is important that we do not confine flourishing in God to roles within the four walls of the church. I heard a story once of a man who worked fairly high up in the healthcare sector. He was offered a significant promotion, which would result in him having substantial impact within his area of influence, yet he wrestled with taking it because he questioned whether climbing the corporate ladder was godly. He believed that in order to be successful as a Christian he should be more focused on serving in the church, aspiring to be an elder. Fortunately, his church leader was able to set him straight, explaining that the world is in desperate need of godly men and women in positions of authority in the marketplace in order to advance God's Kingdom. Success in God is about being the best version of you wherever you have influence. If our motive is to glorify God and our actions honour Him, then it is actually godly to be successful in the church and it is godly to be successful in the marketplace. As leaders it is important that we are intentional about giving those we lead permission to flourish wherever they are.

## MASKS OFF

Taking our mask off as leaders is key to empowering the people around us. Some of us will find it more natural than others, but if we want to make it a priority it is important that we are intentional.

There are various ways we can choose to go after authenticity in our leadership. The suggestions below are not an exhaustive list, but they continue to be helpful principles for me as I learn how to lead without a mask.

1) Pursue a lifestyle of authenticity

The choice to pursue authenticity must first be about you as a child of God gaining your own personal freedom. More important than your title of leader is your title of son or daughter. When you choose to be authentic with your safe people, you are able to deal with orphan thinking and behaviour and grow in revelation of who you really are in Christ. Of course, any breakthrough we receive in our hearts or in our thinking will naturally flow out of us and impact those we are developing. What God does on the inside of us will come out of us to impact the people around us. What is important for us to remember is that the freedom God brings us internally is not first and foremost so that we become better leaders. His ultimate desire in bringing us internal freedom is so that we are able to enjoy our adoption as sons and daughters; so that we are increasingly able to know Him as our Father.

Do you know who your safe people are? Do you have two or three people in your life who know everything about you and still love you? Do you have people cheering you on and holding you accountable for being all God has called you to be? Pursuing a lifestyle of authenticity is important for every follower of Jesus, but it is particularly vital for those of us in leadership. Prioritising authenticity in private means we will be much more likely to leave our masks off when we are leading in public.

2) Let people see your journey

I often find it easier to let people see my journey with God retrospectively: to be honest about something I was struggling with once the struggle is over, to tell them about lies I was believing once I feel secure in the truth, to talk about pain I had to process once the emotion feels less raw, to share about my need for financial breakthrough once the need has been met. It is great when leaders talk openly about the journey God has taken them on, but there is nothing quite like leaders being honest about the journey He *is* taking them on; when they take their mask off in the moment to let those they are leading see who they are as they journey. In my experience as a leader, it has been letting people see my current journey that has most empowered them to go on their own journey with God, to access their own freedom and to step into their own calling.

A few years ago I had the privilege of leading an eight-week TSM course at a church in Oklahoma City, USA. A team of three friends came with me for the first few weeks of the school and we saw many people's lives transformed as God met with us. As part of the launch weekend I spoke about the importance of dealing with disappointment well if we want to live a naturally supernatural life. I shared some of my own story of dealing with disappointment around my battles with sickness and was aware of feeling emotional as I was speaking. I knew when I got to the end of the talk that I still had some disappointment to process. Once I had finished leading everyone else through the process of dealing with their pain, I had a choice. I could swallow my surfacing disappointment until I was home alone later that evening, or I could practise what I had just preached and process my pain in public. I decided to keep my mask off and go for it.

I sat down next to my friend Claire and wept openly about my fear of getting sick again. One of the students on the course came and knelt next to me. She and Claire sat with me as I processed out loud with God, tears flowing down my cheeks. After I had said everything I needed to say, Claire and Kelli prayed for me and I encountered God's comfort and peace. What I love is how my fifteen minutes of public vulnerability gave permission to many other people in the room who saw (and heard) my journey, to more thoroughly express their own pain and disappointment. All of a sudden there was a greater sense of freedom in the room, which flowed through the rest of the course. Kelli became a good friend of mine throughout my trip, and I was able to sit with her on a couple of occasions as she processed her own disappointment from her past. I know that she felt safer to really go for it because she had seen my journey first-hand during the TSM launch weekend.

Are you letting people see your journey with God; the tough bits and the things you are celebrating and feel excited about? Are they aware of current things God is speaking to you about and how you are responding to what He is saying? Do the people you lead know when you need their support; how happy are you to receive it? Allowing people to see your journey and inviting them to pray for you and support you on the way quickly breaks down barriers between you and those you lead. You all get to go on a journey together, empowering each other through mutual support and encouragement to be all God has called you to be.

3) Ask for feedback

One of the things I love about the elders at King's Arms is how quick they are to ask for feedback. I was in a meeting recently and I overheard Simon speaking to one of our interns who had been part of our church family for about four months. He was asking her what she had observed about the church so far, and more specifically if there was anything we could learn from the church she had come from. He wanted to know if there was anything about their culture or the way the church ran that would help us in our growth and development as a church family. I find this inspiring and provoking. It takes a leader secure in their identity to ask an intern for feedback about the church they lead.

I have functioned far too much like an orphan in the past when asking for and receiving feedback. Orphans tend to avoid feedback at all costs because their identity is wrapped up in what they do. Any constructive criticism they receive is likely to be interpreted through the filter of rejection and will probably lead to them feeling rubbish about themselves. As a result, they are likely either to withdraw from what God has called them to do, or work harder in the future to try to please more people. Sons and daughters, however, understand that their identity in Christ is nothing to do with their performance. They realise that constructive criticism does not undermine their value or alter who they are. Rather than avoiding feedback, they welcome it because they see it for what it is: an opportunity to grow and develop in the gifts God has given them.

Asking for feedback as a leader is a great way to intentionally take your mask off. It communicates to the people around you that you do not have all the answers and that you are keen to keep learning and growing. When we ask for feedback from those we lead we give them permission to speak into our lives and we empower them to be part of the solution for our development. As we model asking for feedback, we are much more likely to raise up men and women who understand the value of remaining eager to learn as they lead in their own areas of influence.

Do you have people in your life who regularly give you feedback? Do you receive feedback though the filter of rejection or through the lens of your sonship or daughterhood? Who could you intentionally ask to give you feedback about your leadership? The truth is that none of us is the finished article, and if we ever get to the point of being resistant to feedback we are on a slippery slope. When we are secure in God's steadfast love for us we realise that it is possible to learn from anyone and everyone. Of course, it is not always easy. We have to choose to keep our hearts open to receive input from others, especially people we find challenging, who we would rather judge and keep at arm's length. Yet if our mindset is that we can learn from anyone, and we take time to digest the lessons God is wanting to teach us, our lives and our leadership will be much richer as a result.

4) Be quick to apologise
An 'easy' way to purposely take your mask off as a leader is to be quick to apologise. I say 'easy' because like the other sugges-tions outlined above, apologising makes you vulnerable and can be costly. Yet the benefits of maintained unity and trust in rela-tionships should far outweigh any awkwardness you might feel in the moment.

I have seen the damage done to people who have justifiably looked for an apology from leaders that never came. I have seen the confusion and pain they live with and the resultant internal wrestle they have about their value and worth. I have seen the lack of respect and distrust that grows in their hearts towards those in authority over them. Apologising is rarely enjoyable, but as a leader it is vital if we want to create a spacious place for those we invest in. When we apologise we take our masks off and show the people we lead that we are able to admit we are fallible. This in turn reinforces the truth that anyone and everyone can be used by God.

I have lost track of the number of times I have had to apologise over my years of leadership. I think one of the most challenging moments was when I had to apologise to the youth group I was leading. Apologising to people you deem 'less experienced' than you is always a great test of character! On this particular occasion I had compared goals set by our elders for the church with goals we had set as a youth group. I remember telling our young people how proud I was of them because I felt they had shown more faith in their goals than the leaders of the church. I realised fairly quickly that I had led from a place of pride and had not honoured my elders. Through my leadership I had created an 'us and them' mentality and the fruit of my pride was division.

I decided to pluck up the courage to be honest with my leaders about the mistake I had made and told them I would apologise to the young people when we next got together. The subsequent meeting with the youth and my youth team ended up being one of the most precious times we ever had in God's presence. I took some time to apologise to the young people for what I had said, explaining why it had been wrong. Then we all stood together and took a moment to repent together and to thank God for our leaders and for the privilege of being part of such an amazing church family. God really met with us when we worshipped later that evening. I witnessed first-hand the truth of Psalm 133, that where God sees unity He commands a blessing. The whole experience felt like a defining moment for me as a leader because I saw the relational and spiritual fruit of being quick to apologise.

Would you describe yourself as being quick to apologise with genuine humility in your heart? Ask the Holy Spirit to show you if there is anyone you need to apologise to at the moment and make a decision to take your mask off with them. Heartfelt apology is powerful in the life of a leader. It deepens trust and ensures that connection and unity is maintained. Where God sees unity, He commands a blessing.

Leading without a mask is crucial if we want to empower people to be all God has called them to be. It is certainly not always easy. We risk being misunderstood and having our weaknesses used against us. Yet the freedom those we lead can access as a result of our vulnerability makes any personal cost to us worth it.

How are you doing at leading without a mask?
Are the people you are influencing learning from a distance, or have you invited them to do life with you?
Do those you lead feel permission to show people who they really are: their struggles and their successes?

The truth is that all of us, whether we have led for one week or forty years, are on a journey of learning how to follow Jesus more closely. There will always be lessons to learn, temptations to fight and fears to conquer. None of us have arrived. When we choose to pursue authenticity as leaders we show people that we are disciples, just like them. When we lead without a mask we open the door for those we are championing to access the fullness of life Jesus won for them on the cross.

# 5. GIVE COURAGE WITH YOUR WORDS

If you have ever preached you might be able to relate to the sinking feeling you sometimes get when you discover the piece of Scripture you have been given to speak about. I remember when we did a series at King's Arms preaching through the book of Daniel. We were looking at lessons we could learn from Daniel about how to be ambassadors for God in order to impact the world around us. I knew about the story in Daniel where King Nebuchadnezzar was humbled by God, losing his mind and living like an animal for seven years because of his pride. Honestly, I thought the story was bizarre and had never spent any time studying it. When I found out that this was the chapter I had been allocated to preach on, my immediate response was fear. I was afraid that I would struggle to really get to grips with what the chapter was saying, but as I looked at the passage I realised that God had a lot He wanted to teach us as a church family.

God started to show me what we could learn from Daniel about how to respond as ambassadors to proud and ungodly leadership; specifically that His heart is to see people redeemed rather than removed from their position of authority. The timing of the preach was incredibly prophetic. The Sunday I was due to speak was right after the highly controversial presidential elections in

America. I knew as I was preparing that this preach was going to be prophetic and that it would be significant for us as a church. I also knew that what I was going to say would challenge many in the church to think differently about their response to ungodly leadership and convict some where they were not accurately representing the Father through their behaviour. God clearly wanted to speak through the message I had planned, and yet I woke up on the Sunday morning with a real crisis of confidence. All of a sudden I was plagued with doubts about the material I had prepared, questioning if I had really heard God, and I felt unusually vulnerable and insecure.

No one in the congregation would have guessed that my morning had been such a battle. I preached with real confidence and conviction. It was timely encouragement from one of my elders before the service that brought an end to my internal battle and enabled me to step into freedom. Phil came and prayed for me before the meeting: 'Wendy, you are going to preach with the anointing of a prophet this morning.' He went on to speak truths over me, which one by one silenced my doubts and quashed my insecurities. When he had finished praying, Phil looked me in the eye and told me, 'Go for it this morning, Wendy. Don't hold back. We're right behind you.' Phil's encouragement literally gave me courage to preach with confidence and authority. His words cut across the lies I had been believing and empowered me to fully embrace what God had called me to that morning.[9] What I experienced through Phil's encouragement confirmed what I already knew to be true. The words we speak carry very real power, and as leaders we can strengthen and empower those we lead through what we say.

## WHAT WE SAY MATTERS

The words we speak are powerful. Proverbs 18:21 instructs us that 'The tongue has the power of life and death'. In other words, God has designed it so that what we say really matters. You and I have been created in the image and likeness of God (see Genesis 1:27). In the very beginning as God created the world He spoke things into being that did not previously exist. His words literally created matter and released life, and right now everything is being sustained 'by his powerful word' (Hebrews 1:3). If God wanted to call it a day on the world and stop everything existing at this very moment, He could. He would just need to say the word. You and I are made in our Father's image and likeness, which means that because His words have power, our words have power too. The words we speak have power to release life and hope and to give people courage; they also have power to bring death and despair and cause people to shrink back. What we say matters!

Encouraging people and speaking truth to them is not about giving people warm fuzzy feelings. If we think that encouraging others is namby-pamby and something that we can take or leave as leaders, we have misunderstood the very real weight that our words carry. When we speak words of life over people, something profoundly spiritual takes place. Our words carry within them the power to pull greatness out of the people we lead and empower them to step into all God has called them to. Not only have I seen this at work in my own life, but I have seen it time and time again with the people I invest in. The truth I speak over them and the encouragement I pour into them ignites faith in their hearts for the things God is calling them to. There is no stopping a believer who actually believes that what God says about them is true.

If you have ever read through the book of Proverbs, you will know how frequently Solomon reinforces the truth that our words are powerful. I once gave some of our TSM day-school students the task of pulling out all the verses through ten consecutive chapters that related to our speech. After a twenty-minute period they were still stuck in the first chapter unpacking all the references they had found. Over and over again Solomon instructs us to be mindful of what comes out of our mouth if we want to be wise:

> The words of the reckless pierce like swords, but the tongue of the wise brings healing.
> (Proverbs 12:18)

> Those who guard their mouths and their tongues keep themselves from calamity.
> (Proverbs 21:23)

> Gracious words are a honeycomb, sweet to the soul and healing to the bones.
> (Proverbs 16:24)

If we want to be wise as leaders we need to be intentional with our words; we need to think carefully about what we say and what we choose not to say. Life and death is in the power of your tongue. That is a big responsibility. The words we speak as leaders will either help to create a spacious place for the people we lead, or they will have the opposite effect. We can either intentionally empower people to be all God has called them to be, or inadvertently limit and restrict them, preventing people from fully embracing God's call on their life. What we say matters.

## SEE WHAT THE FATHER SEES

If you are not secure in your identity as a son or daughter of God, you are likely to struggle when it comes to speaking truth or giving encouragement. You may be so focused on getting approval and encouragement from others that you are not even thinking about using your words to spur others on. Or you may genuinely not know how to encourage others because of a lack of encouragement in your own life; you struggle to give away what you have not received.

I remember being told once by a church leader that the way I led offended people. I think he was trying to be encouraging. This was his way of telling me that my life was a provocation to many people. This father in the church is kind and loving. He did not mean me any harm by what he said, but the negative connotations of his choice of words stuck in my heart for a while. I had to actively shake off lies and choose to stand firm in the truth that I am actually a gift to the church. It is possible to think we are being encouraging when actually we are not. Effective encouragement requires careful consideration of the words that we speak and the tone with which we say them.

Some leaders who function with an orphan mentality may shy away from encouraging others because they are nervous about people 'overtaking' them in God. People with the potential of being more gifted than them are seen as a threat because as an orphan their identity is wrapped up in what they can do; they need to be the best. Other leaders might avoid giving encouragement because they do not want to puff people up or cause them to fall into pride. In their minds it is better to limit encouragement and instead focus primarily on a person's weaknesses and areas for development. There are sadly also some leaders who actively discourage those they lead, speaking harsh words that lodge in people's hearts and minds, wounding them for years. The old adage 'sticks and stones may break my bones but names will never hurt me' could not be further from the truth.

When you are secure in God's love for you and you understand who you are as His beloved son or daughter, you take great joy in seeing others flourish around you because of your encourage-ment. You want to see those you lead grow in God and run ahead of you in their gifting, because you know that their success takes nothing away from who you are in Christ. In the Kingdom, their breakthrough is your breakthrough. You are also able to enjoy giving encouragement and speaking truth without the fear of people falling into pride, because you understand that what you are saying is just the tip of the iceberg compared to what God says about the person. As leaders we have the privilege of representing the Father to the people we lead. Our job is to communicate His heart to them; it is His job to sanctify them and convict them if they fall into pride. When you live as a son or daughter, you understand the power of your words to bring life and freedom to the people you influence and, because you understand what the Father says about His sons and daughters, you are able to pass that truth on freely and joyfully.

One of the keys to being a leader who is good at encouraging others and speaking truth is learning to see people through the Father's eyes, to see what He sees. Where we often look at external behaviours and outward appearances and where we tend to filter what we say through judgements we have made, God sees the big picture and looks at the heart. We see this in the way the disciples and Jesus respond differently to the lady who poured the alabaster jar of perfume over Jesus' head. The disciples' response to the woman's act of extravagance was to rebuke her harshly. They did not understand the motivation behind what she did and they saw the poured-out perfume as a waste of money that could have been given to the poor. Imagine if the woman had left the scene with only the disciples' criticism ringing in her ears. She would have left crushed, filled with shame and feeling like she had made a terrible mistake. Jesus' response was entirely different:

> 'Leave her alone,' said Jesus. 'Why are you bothering her? She has done a beautiful thing to me. The poor you will always have with you, and you can help them any time you want. But you will not always have me. She did what she could. She poured perfume on my body beforehand to prepare for my burial. Truly I tell you, wherever the gospel is preached throughout the world, what she has done will also be told, in memory of her.'
> (Mark 14:6-9)

Jesus saw what was going on in the woman's heart and spoke words that were gentle, edifying and life-giving. He looked past the inconvenience of the situation and the money that was 'wasted' and He honoured the woman publicly. Jesus' response ensured that the woman left the scene knowing love and acceptance and hearing the resounding 'well done' of her Saviour. I would love to know what impact Jesus' encouragement in that moment had on the rest of this woman's life. I am sure it was profound.

The words we speak as leaders have huge significance. It is vital that we learn to see what the Father sees in the people He places around us. It is easy to spot the dirt in people's lives and identify people's weaknesses and the areas they need to grow in. It takes a different kind of leader to spot the gold, to see the hidden treasures buried beneath people's shame, fear, character flaws and even pride. Secure sons and daughters of God are not oblivious to the dirt, but they are not fixated on it either. Their primary focus is on calling out the gold in the people they develop, helping them to see themselves as God sees them. This focus does not mean that the dirt is never talked about or that people go unchallenged. The whole of the next chapter is dedicated to the importance of leaders 'speaking the truth in love' (Ephesians 4:15). What it does mean is that spotting the gold takes priority. When we lead like this we show people what their Heavenly Father is like.

## GIVING COURAGE

To encourage someone means to give them courage. I remember reading a book a few years ago, which was written by a man named Banning Liebscher. The whole book was very provoking and inspiring, but one particular section really stood out to me and has stayed with me ever since. Banning writes:

> The main reason why people don't fulfill their destiny
> in God is not a lack of training but a lack of courage.
> I'm increasingly convinced that people don't need more
> training on how to do stuff, rather they need courage to
> do the stuff they already know how to do.[10]

Something resonated in my heart as I read that statement because I knew that it was true. In this day and age we have access to a vast array of quality training at the touch of a button. We can sign up to an online course here or attend a training school there. Where the rubber really hits the road is when it comes to actually putting what we learn into practice. Most often, the reason people do not fulfil their potential in God is not a lack of training but a lack of courage.

Every believer is called by God to have a significant influence on the world around them. All of us carry the mandate to see God's Kingdom extend through us wherever we have influence. The enemy is on a mission to derail us from our destiny by lying to us about who we are and what we are capable of. He comes to undermine our confidence by exposing our weaknesses and amplifying our fears. Training is obviously helpful in giving us the tools we need to fulfil God's calling on our lives, but without the courage to put it into practice, it quickly becomes obsolete. What we are in desperate need of in the church is a culture of encouragement. A culture where from the youngest to the oldest we are taught to use our words to put courage into each other; courage to do the stuff that we already know how to do. As leaders we have the privilege of modelling and establishing this kind of culture in our communities and spheres of influence.

An absence of encouragement results in an absence of courage. If as leaders we do not intentionally encourage those we lead, they are much more likely to give in to fear and much less likely to fulfil their potential in God. Without courage, the people we invest in will avoid taking risks and become too easily settled and satisfied. Conversely, if we create a culture of encouragement where people are believed in and given courage to put the skills and gifts they have into practice, life will flow as a result. People we champion will know the joy of depending on God as they take risks for Him and step out of their comfort zone. They will know the exhilaration that comes from choosing to be courageous in spite of the fear that they feel, and the deep satisfaction that comes from knowing they are doing what God has called them to do. What I find most exciting about a culture of encouragement is the potential it has to change the world. God loves to call us to things beyond our natural capabilities, and He can do incredible things through people filled with courage.

Throughout Scripture we read about men and women doing extraordinary exploits because someone sees what is in them and gives them the courage to go for it. The armour bearer gave Jonathan courage to carry out one of the worst military strategies of all time. After Jonathan had told him the plan, the armour bearer's response was all in: 'Do all that you have in mind ... Go ahead; I am with you heart and soul' (1 Samuel 14:7). I wonder how the story would have played out differently if the armour bearer had told Jonathan what seems glaringly obvious when we read the passage, that his plan was ridiculous and would never work? As it happens, Jonathan and his armour bearer secured a major victory for the Israelites that day.

Then you have Esther, a young girl chosen by God to bring deliverance to an entire nation. Having heard about Haman's plot to eradicate the Jews, she has a private conversation with her uncle Mordecai. Esther knows that the only way to save her people is to approach the king, but she also knows that to approach the king without being invited could result in her being put to death. Her life is literally on the line and understandably she is not keen to take the risk; that is until her uncle gives her courage with his words: 'who knows but that you have come to your royal position for such a time as this?' (Esther 4:14). Mordecai's encouragement of Esther gave her the courage to approach the king uninvited, which in turn led to the plot against the Jewish people being thwarted.

These are just two examples of many throughout Scripture where words of encouragement gave courage to ordinary men and women to fulfil God's call on their lives. Notice that the encouragement was given just at the right time, seemingly ordained by God to be the catalyst for maximum impact. Encouragement is a spiritual activity, not just a self-starting activity. We can ask God for the right words to say at the right time, so that our encouragement propels people into their destiny. Timely encouragement gives people courage and empowers them to step into the adventures God has for them.

Of course, our ultimate goal as leaders is to point people to the Father as their main source of encouragement. We do not want people to depend on us to say the right thing before they will say yes to Jesus. Rather, we want to train them to tune in to the 'well done' of their Heavenly Father, receiving security and courage from Him before anyone else. Having said that, we do have the privilege as leaders of representing the Father to the people we lead. They must not depend on us to empower them to be all God has called them to be, and yet we do have a part to play in their journey. You just never know when your words will be giving courage to the next Jonathan or the next Esther.

## LITTLE COST: LASTING FRUIT

Going out of our way to intentionally encourage someone costs us very little, yet watching the resultant fruit is so exciting. A friend of mine called Sharon is an incredible artist.[11] Not only has she produced some staggering pieces of art, which now hang in the homes of many in our church, she has also been intentional about identifying and encouraging other artists, giving them space to take risks and grow in their gift. What people might not know is that up until the year Sharon did TSM as a student in 2012 she had never put a paintbrush to paper. At university she completed a sculpture degree and so creativity has always been in her blood, but painting felt scary and made her feel vulnerable. I had the privilege of encouraging her and giving her space to take a risk with painting at TSM. You can read some of her story below:

> In order to live out my creative design I needed repeated encouragement because I struggled with so much insecurity and fear. Wendy played a vital role in championing me and giving me space to take risks. As I started to step out in obedience, God showed me step by step what I needed to do, strategies I needed to grow and who

I should work with. As I stepped up and took risks in public, it allowed others to be inspired and identify their gifting, creative and otherwise. There has been an emergence of new artists and creative expressions in recent years at King's Arms, with so much yet to come. There are still days when I forget all that has happened, and I need to remember the promises and the call on my life. Community is vital in this. Just the other day someone I hadn't seen in a while asked me if I was still doing art and provoked me to never stop creating. It was an abrupt but beautiful encouragement to keep going to the next level.

You might be someone who encourages people very naturally and who finds it easy to speak truth to people. Or you might be someone who finds encouraging others awkward and clunky and that speaking truth is something you have to be really intentional about. Wherever you would put yourself on the above scale, all of us can grow as leaders in our ability to give courage to the people around us. Here are some of the keys principles I am mindful of as I look to encourage the people I lead.

1) Understand the extravagant truth the Father speaks over you
It is really difficult to give away what you do not have. In order to be effective at encouraging others and seeing them as God sees them, you first need to go on your own journey of hearing and receiving God's encouragement of you. You need to see yourself through the Father's eyes.

The Bible is full of remarkable truths about who we are in Christ and what God thinks and feels about us. We are 'fearfully and wonderfully made' (see Psalm 139) and we are created in the image and likeness of God (see Genesis 1). God does not deal with us according to our sin, He has compassion on us and loves us with an immeasurable and steadfast love (see Psalm 103). Our Heavenly Father is far from indifferent about us, He rejoices over us with 'loud singing' (see Zephaniah 3, ESV) and His 'goodness and mercy' pursue us every single day of our lives (see Psalm 23, ESV). We are 'without blemish and free from accusation' (see Colossians 1), we are empowered by the Holy Spirit to do the works that Jesus did (see John 14), and the God of the universe promises never to leave us (see Hebrews 13).

These truths, and many more like them, need to get hold of our hearts as leaders. The more we are able to believe these truths for ourselves, the more we will be able to speak them over and pass them on to those we develop. Our encouragement of others flows out of hearing God's encouragement of us. How are you doing at hearing and receiving the 'well done' of your Heavenly Father?

## 2) Be specific

General encouragement is great and definitely worth giving, but when you take the time to be specific with your encouragement it tends to impact people in a deeper way. Instead of stopping at telling someone you are proud of them, tell them why; rather than saying someone did well at a particular activity, unpack what they did well and why it was good; avoid only ever telling people they are generally amazing, instead take time to explain why that is the truth. General encouragement is brilliant, but specific well thought-out words take courage to a whole new level.

It is vital as we think through specific encouragement that we steer clear of only encouraging people for what they do. It often comes more naturally to identify things to encourage based on a person's performance or gifts. I am not saying we should not endorse these things, just that our encouragement should go beyond a person's ability to who they are as an individual. Focusing encouragement solely on performance can reinforce the orphan mentality that someone's value is rooted in what they can do. What we want to do instead is reinforce the truth that a person's value and significance is not based on their performance. They are who they are because of God's grace, because of the irreversible work of the cross in their lives. We want to give people courage about who they are in God and so we must focus our specific encouragement on who people are, not just what they do.

3) Be creative

Encouragement does not have to be limited to just the words we speak. There are a variety of ways that we can be creative with our encouragement that are just as effective at giving courage to people around us.

I remember an occasion when I received a text from one of my elders just as I was leaving my house for work: 'I was just thanking God for you this morning and what a great gift you are to me. That is all!' What the elder did not know is that the previous evening I had spent time with God processing some very deep pain surrounding being single and not having my own family. As I was expressing the pain, I wrestled with lies about how I fitted in the church as a single woman, and I had a fleeting thought of wanting to pack everything in and run away. My elder's encouragement that morning was incredibly timely. It silenced some of the lies in my thinking and gave me courage to keep saying yes to Jesus in the midst of mystery. On the one hand it was just a text that cost my leader very little, on the other hand it was life-giving words that made all the difference to my day.

We can give people courage through the texts or the emails that we send. The great thing about encouraging in writing is that people can go back to what we have said and receive courage multiple times over. I spent a season writing cards of encouragement to my colleagues at the church. Every fortnight I would ask God which two colleagues to write to and then take five minutes to write some truth on a card for them. Again, it cost me very little, but I received multiple messages of thanks indicating that my encouragement had come at just the right time.

We can encourage privately or publicly; in person or through writing; in the church, in our workplaces and even on the streets as we meet people going about their everyday lives. Giving courage to people looks like many different things; all give life and are effective at drawing the best out of those around us. Why not take some time today to think about some creative ways to encourage the people you lead, and see what God does through your words?

4) Have people's backs

I love the way Jesus commissioned His disciples before He went back to be with the Father. Jesus handed the baton of declaring and demonstrating the breaking in of God's Kingdom to His followers. He left them with the mandate to 'make disciples of all nations', 'teaching them to obey everything [He had] commanded [them]'. By anyone's standards this could have been a daunting and overwhelming task, but then Jesus left them with these crucial parting words: 'And surely I am with you always, to the very end of the age' (Matthew 28:20).

Jesus is telling His disciples that He has their backs: 'The task ahead is huge and the responsibility may feel overwhelming, but there is nothing to be afraid of because I am going to be with you. Let that give you courage.' Of course, for all of us, the ultimate reason why we can take courage in any situation we face is because we know that Jesus is with us too. He will never leave us. The God of the universe is backing us up! As leaders we have the privilege of representing the Father to those around us, reminding them of this and communicating to them that we have their backs too. When people we invest in know that we are behind them and we are covering them, it gives them courage and creates a safe place for them to take risks.

I remember one particular TSM evening when I saw this first-hand. One of our students had recently been diagnosed with cancer and we made the decision as a team to pray for her during the evening. It was a costly decision because just a few weeks earlier we lost a very dear friend as a church to cancer. We were all still reeling with the shock of how short our friend's battle had been and one team member in particular, who had been very involved in caring for her right until the end, was still dealing with a lot of trauma.

We decided how we would lead the prayer time and then we went downstairs to connect with the students before the evening got underway. Several minutes later, the member of my team who had just a few weeks before sat with a friend dying of cancer approached me and said she felt God was prompting her to lead the prayer for our student. She said she felt nervous about doing it and that she might end up in tears and not being able to communicate clearly, but it felt important in the midst of her pain and mystery to 'go after cancer again'. I knew that this was a God moment so I told my friend to go for it and that I would have her back; that if she broke down in tears I would be there to take the microphone and lead things forward. It was a privilege to watch the bravery of my teammate that evening and to be able to give her the extra courage she needed to be obedient to Jesus.

What we say as leaders matters. We have the privilege of giving the people we lead courage with our words. Courage to say yes to Jesus, to take risks with their gifts and to embrace God's calling on their lives. Courage to have the influence and impact in the world that God has prepared in advance for them. When we encourage people around us, we fan into flame what God has put in them and who He has called them to be. Whether encouragement comes easy to us, or we have to work at it, the cost to us is minimal compared to the fruit it will produce in those we develop. With our words we can create a safe place for those we are investing in to flourish in God.

How are you doing at releasing life with the words that you speak? Are the people you're leading growing in courage because of what you say to them?

Would you say that you are primarily focused on spotting and drawing out the gold you see in people's lives, rather than the dirt?

Take some time to ask people you lead for feedback about how encouraged or empowered they feel through what you say to them. What do you say that gives them courage, and is there anything you say that detracts from it? Is there something specific you could be encouraging them about in this season of their life? Avoid requesting an immediate response from people. Instead, give them time to think through their answer and then receive what they have to say with an open heart. Being encouraging as a leader is not an optional extra; it is a crucial part of drawing the best out of those God has entrusted to us. What we say really matters.

# 6. SPEAK THE TRUTH IN LOVE

Historically, I have avoided situations where I've had to challenge people. I never really learned how to have healthy, honest conversations as a child and I really dislike 'rocking the boat' or saying things to people that could potentially upset them. My default response has often been to avoid confrontation and hope that things just work themselves out without me having to get involved. As I have grown in my leadership and in my awareness of God as my Father, who gently disciplines me because He loves me, I have come to realise that challenging those I lead when necessary is actually the most loving thing I can do. If I want the people I develop to be all they are called to be in Christ, I have to choose to speak the truth in love.

I remember on one occasion having an older man on my team who was clearly called to be a father in the church. I would watch him as he lovingly interacted with sons and daughters around the room, praying for them and speaking truth to them. It soon became apparent, however, that there were some things he did that stopped him from being fully effective in his calling. I noticed that this particular team member would often focus on praying for women during ministry times and that occasionally he would be overly tactile; giving hugs and showing affection when it was not invited. I knew his motive for expressing love was good, but at times it made me and others feel uncomfortable. My hunch was that if I let things carry on as they were, my friend would inadvertently end up pushing people away, which in turn would inhibit his ability to be the father I knew he was called to be.

The prospect of having a conversation with this team member made me feel sick. I had no idea how to broach the subject and I desperately wanted to avoid crushing my friend or making him feel ashamed in any way. It would have been very easy for me to choose to say nothing and just turn a blind eye, with the hope that things would simply change over time. Yet I knew I had a responsibility as his leader to tell him the truth in love; I genuinely wanted to see this man succeed in his call to be a father to many in the church.

I arranged a time to meet with my friend and his wife, with another guy from my team, to talk about what I had observed and to work out a way forward. I prayed a lot in the lead-up to the meeting, mostly because I was afraid it would all go horribly wrong rather than because I was full of faith for a great outcome. God was incredibly kind as we met together. My friend received what we said with stunning openness and humility, he and his wife took the opportunity to be honest with each other about some key issues impacting their marriage, and the meeting ended with all of us communicating our love for each other. A few days after the meeting, my colleague and I received this email:

A really big thank you for your love and 'tweaks' yesterday. My wife & I felt so loved and secure, and although you had some challenging issues to address we felt honoured and valued by you both. We have been aware of some of the issues for some time but no one has had the courage to address the problems in a way that would help us move on. We really, really appreciate the personal costs that that session cost you both and would want to say how much we love and honour you.

This couple are now flourishing in their walks with God and my friend is truly a father to many, both in his local church and beyond.

I am aware as you read this story that you may have had very different experiences of challenging the people you lead. This is one of my success stories, but sadly it does not always go this well. Often our attempts to confront as leaders are sabotaged by people's pain and insecurities. Whether people respond to our challenge with open hearts or with defensiveness because they feel rejected, speaking the truth in love as leaders is not something we can avoid if we want to lead like Jesus. It is crucial that we are honest with those we are investing in; it is equally crucial that our motivation for doing so is to see them succeed and be all God has commissioned them to be.

## KINDNESS LEADS TO REPENTANCE

I love the way Jesus confronted wrong behaviour. He was never soft on sin and He never turned a blind eye, yet He treated people with dignity and He showed them unconditional love. People corrupted and broken by sin were motivated to change their way of life after they met with Jesus. His kindness led people to repentance; to change the way they thought about God and themselves and to turn away from the things that did them or others harm.

When Zacchaeus met Jesus, he was a corrupt tax collector, focused on taking other people's money for his own gain. Jesus' approach for helping Zacchaeus turn away from his life of sin was not to pretend nothing was happening or avoid him; nor was it to point the finger to accuse or rebuke him harshly. Jesus' strategy for turning Zacchaeus' life around was to pursue him, pick him out of a crowd and stay at his house. Almost immediately Jesus' kindness led to repentance. Zacchaeus chose to give half of his possessions to the poor and pay back money to anyone he had cheated, 'four times the amount' (Luke 19:8).

When Jesus met the woman at the well she was full of shame. The man she was living with was not her husband and she had experienced immense rejection having already gone through five marriages. Yet Jesus had a plan to redeem this precious woman and empower her to be the influencer she was called to be. His plan was not to ignore her or to keep her at arm's length; nor was it to heap more shame on her by exposing her flaws. Jesus' approach for turning this woman's life around was to notice her and ask her for a drink (John 4:7). Jesus' kindness to this woman, along with His stunningly accurate word of knowledge about her life situation, led to her being the catalyst for many in the town she was from choosing to follow Christ.

Jesus' kindness repeatedly led people to repentance. As leaders it is our kindness towards those we are championing that will often be the biggest motivator for change in their lives. We are not meant to be soft on sin or turn a blind eye when we see people operating out of an orphan heart instead of their identity. Equally, we are not meant to respond to sin or orphan thinking with harsh words or judgement. Our role as leaders is to imitate Christ and walk this middle road of speaking the truth to people when we need to, but doing so with God's love in our hearts for them.

## TWO EXTREMES

There are two extremes it is possible to lean towards if you approach confrontation with an orphan mindset. The first is to be very intentional about speaking the truth but forget that you are meant to love the person you are speaking to; that your aim should be to draw the best out of them and empower them to change. If you are not secure in your identity as a dearly loved son or daughter, you may see other people's mess as a bad reflection on you. Your focus then becomes behaviour modification: how can I quickly challenge this person and be honest about how they need to change so that I continue to look good as their leader?

In some cases, leaders who accommodate orphan thinking speak the truth without love because they have never really encountered God's unconditional love personally. They know the theory in their head but they have never experienced God's gentle, tender and grace-filled discipline for themselves. As I have said before, it is very difficult to give away what you have not received. Insecure leaders tend to be harsh and critical in their challenge of others because they are harsh and critical with themselves. God's love has not penetrated their hearts or transformed their thinking enough to convince them that their weaknesses and sin do not change their identity in Christ.

In very extreme cases, highly insecure leaders will regularly challenge the people around them because it will make them feel better about themselves. I was a bully for a number of years while I was at school. Looking back, the reason I was so keen to put others down was because I had such a low opinion of myself. If I could make others feel bad about themselves, I could be distracted from what I really felt about me. In these extreme cases, leaders might not even be concerned about speaking the truth. Instead they will grasp at anything they can to use against those they have authority over in order to bolster their own fragile self-esteem.

When leaders speak the truth to those they oversee but they forget to be motivated by love, a lot of unnecessary damage is done. Those on the receiving end of the challenge are likely to feel squashed and rejected rather than believed in and empowered to change. Some people challenged in this way will turn to self-improvement, working harder to be the person their leader wants them to be. Others will retreat on the inside, listening to and believing lies that tell them they will never amount to much. Either way, people who hear the truth without love will probably struggle to thrive in their walk with God.

The other extreme it is easy to lean towards if you are not secure in your identity is to never challenge anything. This is definitely the end of the spectrum I most naturally gravitate towards. Many leaders wrongly believe that the most loving thing they can do is actually avoid confronting people. They are happy to encourage those they lead, but when it comes to challenging wrong behaviour or speaking truthfully about a person's ability, they would rather bury their head in the sand.

It is common for insecure leaders to get their sense of worth and value from the affirmation and approval of others. If you lead as an orphan, your priority will be that people like you. This means you are likely to shy away from having courageous conversations in case the person you confront develops a negative opinion of you or your leadership. The potential for those you challenge to get upset as a result of what you say could also cause you to steer clear of speaking the truth. If you do speak the truth, tears or hurt expressed by those you challenge will probably reinforce the insecurities you already have about yourself. In order to protect your already weak self-worth, you are likely to conclude that it is better to say nothing.

Some leaders avoid speaking the truth because they have had negative experiences of being confronted by leaders in authority over them. As a reaction to the harsh and critical challenges they have received, they make a decision to 'never be like that in their leadership' and choose instead to lean towards the other end of the spectrum. Sadly, never speaking the truth is an equal and opposite error to speaking the truth without love. When we skirt around difficult conversations and when we fail to communicate clearly, we set those we are developing up for much confusion and disappointment.

I know people in the church and the marketplace who have been left feeling vulnerable and insecure when responsibilities they once had have been taken away from them with no communication. I know other people who have been left confused when they have not been invited to step into leadership opportunities that seemed to make sense for them, with no explanation. I also know people who have been left feeling fearful and unsafe because an individual's inappropriate behaviour in a group setting was left unchallenged by the leader. When we avoid confronting people as leaders we make it difficult for them, and those around them, to grow and develop in their relationship with God.

## TRUTH AND LOVE

There is a middle road we can walk as leaders that flows out of our identity in Christ: refusing to shy away from speaking the truth to those we invest in, but doing so with genuine love in our hearts for them. When we genuinely love the people we lead, we will want to be honest with them because we want them to succeed. When we are secure as leaders we are more able to enjoy the freedom of talking honestly with people about their character, strengths and weaknesses and how they can grow in their gifts. Sons and daughters are less likely to abstain from talking about people's struggles with sin or how their thinking or behaviour needs to change. They understand that speaking the truth in love is God's blueprint for drawing the best out of the people entrusted to them.

Of course, genuinely loving the people we challenge is not always easy. Some people we lead are more difficult to love than others. It can take a lot of prayer and personal sacrifice to really connect with God's love for those we need to confront. Making time to be with God so that we get His thoughts and affections for the people we challenge is crucial if we are going to love them like He does. If we shortcut this process we could easily fall into the error of going through the motions of confronting someone in a loving way but without genuine love in our heart for them. As children of God who are loved unconditionally, we are called to demonstrate a high bar of love for the people we invest in. The more we experience God's love for us, the more we can give it away to others and the more we will be able to challenge people and leave them feeling believed in and empowered.

I remember challenging a friend of mine in a group setting about his reaction to some teaching he had heard. I was facilitating a leadership group and we were reflecting on some material that had been taught the previous week. Most people in the group had positive thoughts about the material, but my friend came across as quite angry as he talked about the preacher and his teaching. I could have just moved on from this leader's opinion and focused on what everyone else had to say, but this felt like a key moment for my friend to get some freedom. My love for this leader motivated me to challenge his comments and find out what was going on in his heart.

I told my friend that I felt his reaction to the speaker seemed a bit extreme and, as a group, we began to ask him some questions to help unpack what he was thinking. I asked him why he was feeling angry and then challenged some misunderstandings he had about what the speaker had said. It turned out that the material had tapped into some unresolved pain my friend was carrying from his past. He had filtered the teaching and the teacher through his pain, which is why he got angry. As a result of our honest conversation and gentle challenge, my friend met up with a mate of his later in the week to process his pain, forgive previous leaders who had hurt him and receive the freedom Jesus won for him.

This was a great moment of us being honest with our friend and him being secure enough to receive what God was highlighting so he could then do something with it. When we speak the truth to people we lead and we have genuine love in our hearts for them, we empower people to change. As an aside, it is really important that as leaders we know our people well enough to be able to assess whether they can handle being challenged in the moment, or whether we need to wait until we see them on their own to share what we observed. If my friend did not feel safe in the group, challenging him in front of everybody would have been more harmful than helpful. There is no substitute for really knowing the people you invest in.

Secure sons and daughters want those they have influence over to succeed in God. They want the people they lead to go further than they themselves ever could in their lifetime. This is true whether you are leading in the church or the marketplace. Speaking the truth in love is an essential skill to learn if we want to lead like Jesus and represent Him well to the people around us. In order to have integrity to speak the truth to others, it is important that we are actively inviting others to do the same to us.

## RECEIVING CHALLENGE

If you lead with an orphan heart you are likely to do all you can to avoid challenge from other people. When people do speak the truth in love, you will probably hear the truth but bypass the love. Truth that is spoken may serve to reinforce the negative opinion you already have of yourself; it will feed your self-rejection. If you cannot escape confrontation, you are likely to be defensive when it comes, justifying your behaviour so that you do not have to admit to areas of weakness. Alternatively, you may respond by agreeing with everything that is said and then proceed to beat yourself up internally for not being perfect in your leadership.

When you are secure in God's love for you and His unchanging opinion of you, you can invite challenge from others and not be rocked by what they say. You can receive the truth with an open heart because you know that what is said does not change who you are in Christ. Our identity is secure, but there is always more for us to learn as we follow Jesus and as we lead others. Receiving challenge well is something we need to practise as leaders. As we give people permission to speak into our lives, we are able to understand ourselves better and we are made aware of potential blind spots in our relationship with God and others. Ultimately, hearing the truth from others helps us to become more like Jesus, which in turn impacts the effectiveness of our leadership.

A friend of mine recently challenged me about getting defensive in a meeting. I had a fairly strong opinion about something and when someone else in the meeting offered an alternative view my response was short and abrupt. She spoke the truth in such a gentle way, yet I still had to fight the urge to justify my behaviour. I took the opportunity to chat with my friend about what she had observed, and as a result we were able to identify why I had been defensive. I had interpreted the person's disagreement with me as them not valuing me. A little bit of orphan thinking was exposed through my friend's challenge, and it has been hugely helpful in enabling me to respond differently to disagreements in subsequent meetings.

Do you lead in such a way that communicates to those around you that you are open to being challenged? When was the last time someone confronted you, and how did you respond? Of course, the complication for us as leaders is that there will inevitably be times when those who challenge us do not speak the truth, or they challenge us out of their own brokenness and pain rather than out of love. In these times we do not need to be rocked in our leadership and we do not need to go on the defensive. As secure sons and daughters we can listen to the person's challenge, validate their feelings even if we disagree with what they say or how they say it, and thank them for their courage in sharing their heart with us. This is not always easy and we are all on a journey, but it is great truth to remember as we grow in our identity as children of God. Learning to receive input from others as leaders is crucial if we want to create a culture where people naturally speak the truth to each other.

## APPEAL TO IDENTITY

When we speak the truth to people, it is so important that we remind them who they are in Christ rather than just focusing on trying to modify their behaviour. We need to appeal to people's identity in order to empower them to change. Rather than leaving people solely with the behaviours they need to stop or start, our aim should be to leave people with the truth about who they are. What people think about themselves will directly impact how they behave. It appears to me that most of the situations we need to challenge as leaders come about because people are believing lies about their identity. If we can help people to change their thinking about themselves so that it is more in line with what God thinks, their behaviour is likely to follow suit.

When it comes to sin, the best way to help people step into freedom is to appeal to their identity. Rather than focusing on the behaviour the person wants to stop, we need to remind them of who they are in Christ. We need to teach them the truth that they are actually 'dead to sin' (Romans 6:11) and hardwired to want to please God because they are a '[slave] to righteousness' (Romans 6:18). 'This is who you are now because of Jesus!' should be the cry that bubbles up from our hearts as we disciple people living lives that do not reflect their sonship or daughterhood. We need to remind people who they are, obviously without a hint of con-demnation and full of kindness so that they are led to repentance.

When we speak to people about their gifts and calling, it is equally important that we appeal to their identity. The truth is that we are sons and daughters of God irrespective of our gifts and abilities. We are not what we do. Reminding people of this truth will help them to stay secure as we talk about weaknesses they need to work on or areas they need to grow in. Appealing to identity will also prevent people shying away from the unique call of God on their lives. Jesus tells us that we are the light of the world and that we should not hide our light under a bowl (see Matthew 5:14). When we understand who we are, we are more likely to fulfil the purpose God has for our lives.

Although we are called as leaders to challenge those we lead, ultimately it is not our job to change them. We cannot be responsible for making people more like Jesus; that is the Holy Spirit's job. What we can do is pray. Our prayers are 'powerful and effective' (James 5:16) and as we pray for the people we invest in, often God will work in their hearts in a way that pre-empts conversations we need to have with them. It is the Holy Spirit's job to 'convict the world of sin' (John 16:8, NKJV) and He is really good at it. It is also the Holy Spirit who 'testifies with our spirit' that we are children of God; He is the one who brings revelation to us of our identity in Christ (Romans 8:16). As we speak the truth in love, it is key that we appeal to people's identity; it is then up to the Holy Spirit to bring revelation that empowers people to change.

## SPEAKING THE TRUTH IN LOVE

We have established that healthy confrontation is a key skill for us to learn as leaders in order to draw the best out of those we develop. As well as inviting challenge ourselves and being secure in our identity, there are a few other pointers that will help us as we embark on this journey of speaking the truth in love.

1) Learn from Jesus

In Matthew 18:15 Jesus gives us some helpful guidelines when it comes to confronting people: 'If your brother or sister sins, go and point out their fault, just between the two of you. If they listen to you, you have won them over.' The context of this instruction is confrontation because of a person's sin, but there are principles here that can apply to any kind of challenge.

The first thing we can learn is the importance of confronting people face-to-face. Jesus instructs us to go to the person. Challenging people over text or email is never going to turn out OK. You cannot hear people's tone or read their facial expressions. Also written challenge can be read and re-read, it is very permanent and often damaging. At King's Arms we have this philosophy, 'encourage in writing, challenge in person'. When we live by this principle it prevents a lot of unnecessary heartache. Notice also that Jesus encourages us to talk about the sin exclusively to the person who has committed it. Sadly, if we are not secure in our identity what we tend to do is talk to lots of other people about the sin but never confront the person who committed it. Jesus places a high value on us covering each other's weaknesses.

I love that the scripture specifies we should point out our brother or sister's fault, singular, and that our motivation for speaking to them should be to win them over. Confrontation is not an excuse to list off everything that frustrates us about the person we are speaking to, or to get things off our chest by having a good rant. God 'keeps no record of wrongs' and neither should we (1 Corinthians 13:5). Before we go to the person, it is important that we deal with any unforgiveness in our heart towards them so that we can genuinely love them when we tell them the truth. As far as Jesus is concerned, confronting people is about winning them over so that they refuse to settle for anything less than what God has for them. How are you doing at following Jesus' guidelines as you challenge those you lead?

2) Seek first to understand, then to be understood
This is a particularly helpful tool for leaders who are quick to speak

the truth but sometimes forget the importance of loving the person they are speaking to. The statement comes from the book, *The 7 Habits of Highly Effective People*,[12] and focuses on the importance of listening well when communicating with others. Being mindful of this principle stops us having an 'all guns blazing' approach to confrontation. Instead, it encourages us to press the pause button on the things we want to say, so that we can prioritise understanding what is going on for the person we are challenging.

I remember asking a guy I was investing in if he would do an announcement at church one Sunday morning. My reason for asking him was to give him a platform to grow and develop in his leadership, specifically around casting vision to the whole church. His response when I had the conversation with him was disappointing. He very quickly refused the opportunity, telling me it was my job to do that particular announcement. I felt confused and upset by his unwillingness to step up and I knew that I needed to have a follow-up conversation with him.

It would have been easy for me to initiate the conversation by sharing how difficult I had found his response, but I wanted to start by understanding what had been going on for him that morning. I asked him to help me understand why he responded the way he did when I asked if he would do the announcement. My friend thought for a moment and then very honestly told me that he had reacted out of fear. As the realisation of what had happened dawned on him he was very quick to apologise.

Understanding my friend's heart immediately softened my response to him. It enabled me to bring the challenge that was necessary with grace and acceptance. I was honest with my friend about how his response had made me feel and how I wished he had responded differently. I was also able to ask how I could help him in the future to not give in to fear when leadership opportunities opened up. We had a great conversation that helped my friend grow in self-awareness and helped me feel confident again about the leadership call on his life. Had I approached the confrontation wanting to get my point across first, the outcome could have been very different. Seeking first to understand before you are understood is a great tool in drawing the best out of those you are raising up.

3) Say the last 10 per cent

If, like me, you are most comfortable avoiding confrontation, you will need to be intentional about booking in meetings to have honest conversations with people. If intentionally booking in meetings is the first step on your journey of embracing confrontation, the second step is making sure you say everything that you need to say.

It is so easy once you are in the middle of a meeting, face-to-face with the person you need to challenge, to neglect to say what you actually need to say. In the pressure of the moment it is possible to give in to fear, and fumble the reason that you called the meeting in the first place; skirting around the issue that you need to address but never really talking about it. It is easy to think that you are confronting someone when actually you are not.

A great way to combat this temptation of challenging someone without really challenging them is to write down the last 10 per cent. Ask yourself the one thing you must make sure you say to the person before the meeting is over, then write it down and take it into the meeting with you. The last 10 per cent is usually the most uncomfortable thing you need to say, but making sure you say it is the most loving thing you can do for the person you are speaking truth to.

4) Recognise that God is ultimately responsible for people

Even if we embrace everything outlined above and we do a brilliant job at confronting someone, the likelihood is there will be times when those we challenge respond badly and feel crushed because of their own orphan thinking. In these moments we have to take comfort in the fact that God is responsible for them and He is committed to looking after them.

As long as we have done all we can to speak the truth in love, we cannot be responsible for people's responses to our challenge. This is particularly important to remember for leaders with a high level of empathy. Empathy enables you to put yourself in another person's shoes and connect with how they might feel in any given situation. The great thing about empathy is that it enables you to love people really well. The downside is that it can easily lead to over-responsibility for people, resulting in watered down confrontation as you attempt to protect people's feelings. As we seek to speak the truth in love, it is important to remember that God is ultimately responsible for the people we lead. We have to trust their emotions and responses to Him.

Speaking the truth in love is not always straightforward, but it is a privilege. It enables us to be more like Jesus in our leadership. We get to show those we invest in where their thinking or behaviour is not in line with who they are in Christ. We are also able to reveal God's kindness through what we say and how we say it, and empower those we challenge to pursue all they are called to be. There is something very special about seeing the people you champion succeed because you have challenged them on something and they have felt enabled to change.

Some of us will confront people very naturally. It will flow out of our sonship and daughterhood and we will be able to draw on our experiences of excellent role models who have spoken the truth to us. Others of us will need to go on a journey of correcting wrong thinking about confrontation and processing pain from bad experiences we have had of being challenged by others. We will need to practise being honest with those we lead, asking them for feedback as we do so that we can develop and grow.

Asking for feedback obviously takes a lot of courage, but it is a brilliant way to learn. A friend of mine often went back to her colleagues a few days after she had confronted them to ask for feedback about how they felt the conversation had gone. She asked them what she had done that was helpful and what they had found difficult. A huge benefit of this follow-up conversation was the way it enabled my friend to see where her colleagues had misinterpreted things she had said. Not only did my friend learn about her confrontation skills, she was also able to deal with misunderstandings that could have caused further difficulty. My friend's ability to lead with such humility is a real provocation to me.

How would you rate your ability to speak the truth in love to those you are developing?

Is your challenge to be more intentional about speaking the truth, or do you need to prioritise more time with Jesus so that the truth you are already speaking comes with genuine love and kindness? Are there conversations you need to book in to have with people as a result of reading this chapter?

Speaking the truth in love is not something we can take or leave as leaders. It is a vital part of our role in seeing the people God has entrusted to us flourish. Speaking the truth combined with loving the individual is a really powerful tool in the hand of a leader.

# 7. GIVE RESPONSIBILITY AND SPACE

When I think back to how quickly I was released to lead, such a short space of time after I had given my life to Jesus, I am amazed. I was entrusted with responsibility way before I felt I was ready. I do not have many detailed memories of those early days of leadership. Maybe I blocked a lot of them out because of how awkward and uncomfortable it felt to be so far out of my comfort zone. What I do recall is how much fear and insecurity I had to wrestle with every time I was given an opportunity to lead.

I remember a time I was asked to co-lead worship at a small group I was part of. I had taught myself the guitar as a student. I knew about four or five chords and my strumming was pretty good, but I had absolutely no confidence in my ability to sing. The thought of singing in public made me feel sick. When my group leader invited me to lead alongside him I felt terrified. It would have been so easy for me to turn down the opportunity, but instead I decided to give it a go. It was my leader's encouragement of me and his belief in my ability that gave me the courage I needed.

I have fractured memories of the actual evening. I remember everybody standing in a circle to worship and me standing opposite my leader, who was also playing a guitar, so that I could look at how he played each chord. Before the evening started I told my leader that he would need to sing really loudly because I was un-likely to sing at all. I remember how difficult it was to form chords with the fear-induced sweat that quickly covered my hands, and the immense sense of relief I felt when the whole 'ordeal' was over.

I have led worship many times since that first awkward and clunky experience. These days I love to facilitate worship when there is no official worship leader: singing out songs, sharing prophetic contributions with confidence and hosting God's presence. I felt like a rabbit in headlights so many times in my early years of leadership. Yet, when I look at where I am now and the leadership influence I am privileged to have, I am so grateful for the people who took chances with me. I am indebted to the leaders around me who drew me out of my comfort zone and believed in me before I had any belief in myself.

Our words of encouragement as leaders are vital if we want to see people be all God has called them to be, but our encouragement goes to a whole new level when we actually give people responsibility; when we create space for them to try new things and have a go. When we invite those we are investing in to take responsibility and we give them opportunities to lead we communicate that we believe in them and that we trust them. Trust is a great antidote for self-doubt and a powerful motivator when it comes to drawing the best out of people. The more secure we are in our sonship or daughterhood, the more comfortable we will feel to delegate leadership to those we are raising up.

## JESUS' EXAMPLE

Jesus is the master when it comes to entrusting people with responsibility. When I read about the journey He took His disciples on and the way He sent them off in pairs to proclaim and demonstrate the Kingdom, I feel provoked. I know I would have been reluctant to send them off on their own so early; surely they needed some more thorough training? Jesus gathered a group of very average men, who for the longest time did not comprehend who He was, let alone what He was calling them to do. They struggled to understand Jesus' teaching, made mistakes during ministry and argued about who was the most important. To say that they had a lot to learn is an understatement.

Yet Jesus sent the disciples out really early on in their training to do what He had been doing. He entrusted them with responsibility and gave them space to try new things, and because He did, they grew. Had I been the one sending the disciples out, I think I would have followed them at a reasonable distance so that I could keep an eye on exactly what they were doing. This would mean I could give immediate feedback to the disciples on their technique in proclaiming and demonstrating the Kingdom. It would also enable me to quickly clear up any mess they might get themselves into. Jesus did not go with His disciples (see Luke 9:1-6;10). Instead, He trusted them to do what He was asking them to do. Although there were many mistakes made along the way and much feedback needed, Jesus continued to entrust His disciples with responsibility. He empowered them so much that when they were filled with the Holy Spirit at Pentecost there was no stopping the advance of God's Kingdom.

My challenge when it comes to giving people responsibility is managing my expectations of where I think they should be on their journey before I release them. I tend to expect them to be nearer my level of leadership before I give them space to lead, forgetting that I was nowhere near where I am today when I started leading in my late teens. The truth is that being given responsibility before we feel ready is part of how we grow. I have made so many mistakes in my leadership over the years, but I am a better leader now because of them. In fact, one of the main ways I have grown as a leader has been through getting things wrong and deciding to do things differently next time round. Being encouraged to lead before we are ready also teaches us what it looks like to lean into Jesus. There is nothing better than feeling out of your depth to strengthen your dependence on God. If we can equip those we lead to be fully reliant on Him, anything is possible.

If we want to empower the people we invest in to be all they are called to be in God, we have to be intentional about entrusting them with responsibility and creating space for them to experiment with their gifts. The more secure we are in our identity as sons and daughters the easier this will be, because our value is not wrapped up in our or others' performance. There are various ditches we are likely to fall into if we lead with an orphan mindset, which will have a negative impact on those we are eager to release. The more we are aware of these ditches, the more we can intentionally avoid them. The more we avoid them, the more those we are raising up will feel trusted and able to grow.

## REALLY GIVE RESPONSIBILITY

If you are not secure in your identity as a son or daughter of God, you are likely to find it hard to give people responsibility, especially if you see a person as more gifted than you. Orphan thinking tells us that our significance is wrapped up in what we do: that if someone is better than us at something it somehow takes away from who we are. When a person comes along who has the potential to be better than us at a particular role, they pose a threat to our value and we will be nervous about them being released.

If we do manage to give people responsibility, we are likely to struggle to be open-handed and really give the responsibility away. We might communicate to someone that we want them to take the lead in a particular project, and yet still want to have input in every decision that is made. If your identity is in your performance rather than your sonship, your reputation will be wrapped up in how you perform, but also how those you lead perform. As a result, you will be keen to keep a close eye on everything that is done by those you have 'delegated' to. In some cases you might resort to taking responsibility back, 'just in case' circumstances do not play out as you would like. This kind of leadership does not communicate trust and it is not empowering.

I remember asking one of my interns to host a time of worship at TSM. I was in the room and available to assist her whenever she needed it, but I was confident in her ability to do a good job. I was feeling slightly on edge that morning. We had a visiting speaker with us who is well known among our family of churches. It was his first time with us and I was keen to make a good impression. The desire to impress people, as opposed to pleasing God, is never a good foundation to lead from. I was about to find out the hard way.

Worship was going well until we got to one particular contribution. One of our students, who was clearly going through a difficult time, came to the microphone to sing a prophetic song. The atmosphere of faith in the room quickly vanished as our student sang about all her hardships and troubles. I exchanged anxious glances with my intern and made an executive decision that I needed to step in and take the lead. I walked towards the microphone in an attempt to hurry the song through to its completion. When the song was over I took some time to speak truth to the students to help fix our eyes back on Jesus. It did not take long for the atmosphere of faith in the room to be restored. I took more of a back seat again and worship continued.

Within a few minutes the Holy Spirit had convicted me of what I had done. 'You gave the responsibility of hosting to your intern,' He said. 'You took the responsibility back because you were nervous about what that leader would think. Your intern might have led the situation exactly like you did if you had given her the opportunity to have a go.' His tone was gentle and patient but I was totally undone. I had been more interested in maintaining my reputation with a visiting speaker than empowering and releasing my spiritual daughter.

At the end of the session I pulled my intern to one side and apologised to her for taking back the responsibility I had entrusted to her. When I asked what she had been planning to do at the end of the negative prophetic song, she told me she was going to do almost exactly what I did. I learned some valuable lessons that day. Firstly, that my identity was more wrapped up in performance than I thought it was. Secondly, that leading for the praise of people rather than the pleasure of God is a rocky foundation. Thirdly, that when you entrust responsibility to someone it is important that you really give it them.

I am not saying that when we delegate responsibility to others we should have no involvement in what they do, or never intervene or comment. I talk about the error of absence in leadership later in this chapter. Being a good leader is about creating a safe place for the people we are investing in to be all God has called them to be. In order to do that it is important that we are present. Yet there is a big difference between being present because you want to support and build on what the leader is already doing, and being present because you are insecure and you want to be in control.

In order to effectively empower the people I give responsibility to it helps me to think of myself as being part of their team. Seeing myself in this way motivates me to be present, with the specific focus of encouraging and serving the emerging leader whilst also being available to back them up if things go wrong. Thinking through the lens of team also reminds me that I have permission to contribute and comment, making the most of key opportunities to offer my leadership expertise when I think it will be helpful. In order to be fully releasing as leaders we do not have to keep quiet or be absent. What we do have to do is learn to discern the moments it is appropriate for us to say something and when it is right to withhold our input and let things carry on as they are.

There may be the odd occasion when you need to actually take responsibility back from someone you have delegated to. I remember a colleague of mine having to do this once. She had entrusted the organisation of an event to one of her team, but it quickly became apparent that the team member was not competent. My colleague took the responsibility back to ensure that the event happened and that those expecting to attend were served well. In this scenario she made a great leadership decision. Sometimes this kind of action is necessary; however, even when it isn't I have often found myself micromanaging people I have given responsibility to. I can remember many times over my years of leadership completing tasks I have asked my team to do, not because I had to, but because of insecurity in my heart.

God has been very kind in bringing me freedom as I have learned from my many mistakes over the years. Giving people responsibility is now one of my favourite things to do. I am certainly not perfect at it. There are often occasions when I have to very deliberately choose not to say anything so that the people I am raising up can make their own decisions and learn from their mistakes. There are also some occasions when I intervene unnecessarily and I have to go back to people to apologise for not letting them take the lead. A helpful question I try to ask myself when discerning whether I need to assist in a situation or not is, 'What's the worst that could happen if this carries on as it is?' What I am learning is that God is much more comfortable with the potential mess and unpredictability of giving away responsibility than I am.

## ALLOW PEOPLE TO BE THEMSELVES

When David decided to take on Goliath, King Saul was keen to equip him for the task: 'Then Saul clothed David with his armour. He put a helmet of bronze on his head and clothed him with a coat of mail, and David strapped his sword over his armour' (1

Samuel 17:38-39, ESV). Yet David could not fight Goliath in Saul's armour. David was used to fighting, but not laden with armour or wielding a sword. Saul's way of doing things did not fit David. He had to be himself as he went into this battle. 'Then he took his staff in his hand and chose five smooth stones from the brook and put them in his shepherd's pouch. His sling was in his hand, and he approached the Philistine' (1 Samuel 17:40, ESV). The rest is history.

It is so important when we give responsibility that we release people to be fully themselves. It can be tempting instead to shape the people we develop to be mini versions of us: to want them to think like us, execute tasks like us, and plan and prioritise like us. This is particularly true if we lead out of insecurity. People who operate like us are easier to understand and, therefore, easier to lead. They pose less of a threat to our leadership because they are less likely to rock the boat with different opinions and ways of doing things. Yet God calls us to a different kind of leadership from what we see modelled by Saul. Rather than wanting people to wear our armour, sticking with what is familiar to us, we are to release people to find their stones and to use their slingshots. We are to celebrate people's uniqueness, seeing their differences as a blessing rather than a threat, and empower those we champion to find the best way of leading for them.

Philbe and I have served alongside each other in leadership for many years. We started out being part of the youth team together and more recently we have been on the leadership team for TSM. We are very different, in too many ways for me to mention here, and I would be lying if I said that our differences had never been a cause of frustration and challenge for both of us. I am sure there have been multiple times when I have tried to get Philbe to wear my armour. Yet as we have journeyed in leadership together, I have learned to celebrate the ways she is different to me and increasingly champion her being who God has made her to be. I can honestly say that my life and the things we have led together are richer because she has been part of the team. She has taught me so much.

One of the ways Philbe and I are different is to do with how we write talks. Philbe is a great teacher, but the way she chooses to write her talks makes absolutely no sense to me. I like to write my material on my laptop in a Word document, with headings and subheadings and page numbers and order. Philbe prefers to take a blank sheet of paper and write her talks with a pen in cloudlike bubbles around the page. She assures me that there is some sort of flow to the material, although I think I would struggle to see it if I were to look at the finished product! This is Philbe's slingshot and stones. I could insist that she wear my armour and write talks the same way I do. However, boxing her like that would mean we would miss out on experiencing the very best version of her when she teaches.

Of course, releasing people to be themselves does not mean there is no need for us to train those we are raising up. Passing on skills and lessons we have learned through our leadership experience is a key component of enabling people to grow. I find it helpful to look at this training through the lens of principles versus preferences. In other words, what are the key principles it would be helpful for everybody who wants to grow in leadership to learn, and what are just my own personal preferences in any given situation? Where principles are universally applicable, preferences are unique to individuals and so should not be used in a prescriptive way when training others. When it comes to writing talks, for example, key principles could include things like starting the talk with vision so that people want to listen to what you are going to say, and the importance of self-disclosure. Preferences could relate to things like how you write your talk, how you structure your talk, and the use of visual aids or props to reinforce your material. Training those we give responsibility to is hugely important, but not at the expense of them losing who they are.

## CONTROL VERSUS ABSENCE

The other end of the spectrum when it comes to struggling to really give people responsibility, is readily entrusting leadership to others but without the necessary oversight for them to grow. Just as it is possible for families to have fathers and mothers who are absent, who do not provide the covering their children so desperately need, the same can be true of leadership in the church or workplace. In our desire to empower those we invest in to feel completely free to run with their responsibilities, we can inadvertently fall into the error of absence.

Whenever I am tempted to be absent in my leadership, it is often in response to a fear of being seen as controlling. As an aside, I think this can be a challenge that women in particular face in their leadership. Women who are gifted leaders can often be misunderstood and have to wrestle with the lie that if they are assertive in their leadership they are trying to usurp authority. One of the main fears I come across in my interactions with women, which holds them back from leading within the church, is the fear of being seen as pushing themselves forward. 'I don't want to be seen as trying to take authority,' is a common reason why women hold back, choosing to keep their opinions to themselves rather than speaking them out. The enemy has done a great job at disempowering women in the church by telling them that when they lead they are being controlling; that their strength is rooted in the spirit of Jezebel. Of course, there are some women in leadership who do operate out of control – I have done it myself over the years – but the truth is that the spirit of Jezebel is not gender-specific. As leaders in the church, we need to give permission to and create space for men and women to be all they are called to be.

Absence in leadership can also stem from leaders reacting to where they have been controlled in the past. If you have experienced the suffocating effects of controlling leadership, you are likely to want to stay completely out of the way when you give responsibility to others. Your motivation for doing so is to give them the space that you never had but so desperately wanted. It is easy to think that in order to give people the best chance of growing and developing we have to be totally hands-off when it comes to the responsibilities we give them. Yet absence is not the solution to control.

I remember visiting a church to speak at their Sunday morning service and during the time of worship suddenly feeling very anxious. I do still get nervous when I speak, but the intensity of the anxiety that morning was surprising. I discerned fairly quickly that what I was feeling was not to do with me, but that I was picking up an atmosphere in the room. When one of the ladies on my team communicated that she was also sensing a lot of anxiety, I started to ask God what was going on.

As I looked around the room God started speaking to me about there being a lack of confident fathers and mothers in the church. The leader of the church happened to be away on sabbatical at the time. Although there were other leaders in place to take responsibility that morning, they seemed to be unsure about their roles and the level of authority they carried. The internal wrestling and insecurities of these leaders resulted in a general sense of nervousness and anxiety in the atmosphere. The father of the house was absent and it had a tangible impact on the feel in the room. Of course, it was not wrong for the leader to be away on sabbatical, although it did illustrate to me again the importance of raising up secure sons and daughters. God drew my attention that morning to the possible corporate impact of insecure leadership in the church, of a lack of fathers and mothers. Being secure in our identity and present as fathers and mothers is crucial if we want to see those we entrust with responsibility succeed.

Another reason some leaders choose to be absent is because their primary focus is on protecting their own reputation rather than covering their sons and daughters. If you are not secure in your sonship or daughterhood, your reputation is likely to be wrapped up in how well those you delegate to perform. You may readily give people responsibility, but you will quickly be hands-off so that if things go horribly wrong it will not reflect badly on you. If those we delegate to do not perform as well as we had hoped, we might further protect our reputation by making comments like 'what a shame, I thought they were more gifted than that' or 'I guess they weren't as ready as I thought'. Secure leaders understand that their reputation is nothing to do with people's performance. Their identity in Christ enables them to take the flak for any mistakes made by those they delegate to, whilst at the same time allowing their trainees to take the credit for their successes. People we release into leadership need to know that we have their backs and that we will not be rocked by their successes or their failures.

The truth is that absence in leadership can create just as much insecurity and uncertainty for those we champion, as leadership that is full of micromanaging and control. People we lead need to be covered and coached; they need to be given constructive feedback and to know that we are cheering them on. If we are absent in our leadership, it can actually hinder the growth of those we invest in because they may not feel safe. It is finding this sweet spot of really giving people responsibility but doing so under the security of our covering and coaching that enables people to really flourish in God.

## SWEET SPOT

It is crucial that we learn how to really give people responsibility and space to grow in God, without controlling them or throwing them in at the deep end with no support. There are no set formulas when it comes to developing and empowering others. Everyone is wired differently, and what works for one person might not necessarily work for another; that is why knowing our people as leaders is so important. Phil Wilthew, one of our elders at King's Arms, has written a great book called *Multiplying Disciples*.[13] In it there is a really helpful tool that can be used for training and releasing those we lead. It outlines an easily replicable process, which I have found effective in equipping people on many occasions. As with any leadership tool, the phases are there to serve you and those you are investing in, rather than to constrain or inhibit you.

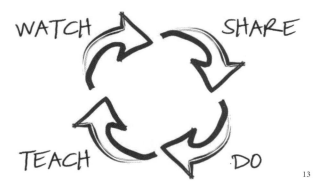

13

1) Watch it

Invite the person you are training to watch how you do a particular task. Encourage them to actively observe what you do: how you start the activity, different things you say or do during it and how you end what you are leading. Ask your trainee to note down questions or comments they have about what they have observed. Then at the end of the task, carve out time to talk these through together.

It is so important that the people we raise up do not just learn how we do something. They also need to understand the heart behind why we do what we do. Taking time to discuss their observations and questions provides an opportunity for the information and thought processes we instinctively have in our heads to be passed on to others. This practice ensures that the people we lead don't just copy our behaviour, but that they understand the reasoning and vision behind our leadership. I have found these discussion times helpful for me personally in growing as a leader. When you are asked questions about why you do things a certain way, it provokes you to look at your leadership with fresh eyes. Sometimes I have changed my approach to situations off the back of questions I have been asked by those I am investing in.

2) Share it

Invite the person you are training to share the delivery of the task with you. Meet with them ahead of the event to plan together what you are going to do and to decide who is going to take responsibility for each part. Make sure you have plenty of time to prepare and to practise the activity. At the end of the event, book in time to talk through how everything went. Give your trainee lots of encouragement and helpful feedback for how to tweak things next time they have an opportunity to lead.

Giving feedback is an important skill to learn as a leader. I have friends who used to dread the feedback they were given because they knew the tone would be critical and the focus would always be on what they needed to improve. Other friends have communicated desperation for feedback because nothing has ever been said about their leadership. With a vacuum of information they have been left to guess what they do well and how they need to develop, which has resulted in uncertainty and insecurity.

I do not get it right every time, but my practice when it comes to giving feedback is to start by asking the person I am developing how they feel things went. In my experience, people are generally very quick to identify areas that they need to improve, so I often specify that the person start their feedback with what they think went well. After I have heard their thoughts, I tailor my feedback accordingly. If my trainee has struggled to identify anything positive about what they did, I will spend more time encouraging them than giving suggestions for improvements. If they cannot identify any areas for growth, I will still encourage them, but also make sure I share one or two suggestions for how they might develop their leadership for next time.

I tend to limit my suggestions for improvement to just one or two things at a time. Any more than that and people will struggle to really implement change. I also aim to focus constructive feedback on leadership principles rather than my own leadership preferences. Sometimes I just encourage those I am giving feedback to and I choose not to mention any areas for them to improve. I find that this is a great way to reinforce the truth that their identity is not rooted in their performance. I also try to be mindful of celebrating people's obedience over the outcome of their leadership. In other words, if they have stepped out in something because they felt Jesus tell them to and it all went horribly wrong, my priority is to celebrate their obedience over rectifying their mistakes.

3) Do it

You might repeat the 'share it' section of this tool multiple times, depending on the gifting and confidence level of the person you are raising up. The third stage is to empower your trainee to take full responsibility for shaping, planning and executing the task on their own, with minimal involvement from you. The ideal scenario is for you to be available to coach in the lead-up to the event where necessary, but to have no intervention when the activity is actually happening. This is easier said than done. I have lost track of the number of times I have had to 'sit on my hands' and intentionally keep my mouth shut in order to let those I am raising up make their own decisions and learn from their own mistakes.

It is important to book in time after the event to talk through how everything went. Again, start by asking your emerging leader how they think they did. Asking for their thoughts first, rather than jumping straight in with our feedback, helps those we are raising up to grow in self-awareness. We have already looked at the importance of leaders going on this journey. The more we know who we are, the more we can grow in our security as sons and daughters. Good self-awareness also enables us to understand and, therefore, lead others more effectively. Once the person you released has shared their perspective on what they did, it is for you to offer your observations. Give lots of encouragement as well as communicating your honest feedback so that there is plenty of opportunity for learning and development.

4) Teach it

The last stage in the cycle is releasing the person you are training to take someone else through the above process. A great way to identify if your new leader has really taken on board what you have imparted to them is if they are able to pass on to someone else what they have learned. Those you are investing in might stay in the 'do it' stage for a while before they move on to this section, but empowering them to pass their skills on to others is ultimately what you are aiming for. As you watch them train others, you can take a step back and celebrate how God has used you to give someone responsibility and space to grow and develop.

One of our greatest privileges as leaders is to see those we invest in come alive as they comprehend who God has called them to be and embrace what He has called them to do. When you are secure in your identity as a child of God, you are able to celebrate when people overtake you in God; in fact, this becomes your aim. When you understand that other people's success takes nothing away from your value or significance, you get excited about giving people responsibility and space to grow in their gifts. You also understand the value of being present as people develop, offering insight and coaching to help them thrive as they step out in obedience to God.

How are you doing at really giving people responsibility and space to grow in their gifts?

Do the people you are investing in feel free to make their own decisions as they grow in their leadership, even if that means they make mistakes?

Are you staying present as you release people so that they can learn from your experience and you can give constructive feedback for their development?

None of us is going to be perfect on this journey of really releasing people without falling into the error of absence. What we can do is apologise quickly when we get things wrong and at the same time refuse to back off from intentionally releasing and empowering those God has entrusted to us. Why not ask the Holy Spirit what your next step is when it comes to being a leader who gives responsibility and space to those around you? Then go on a journey of being led by Him as you navigate practically the outworking of what He says.

# 8. REDEFINE SUCCESS AS OBEDIENCE

Leading worship takes a lot of courage, especially when you are introducing the congregation to a song you have written. I remember hosting a Sunday morning meeting when one of our worship leaders started a time of worship with one of his new songs. Honestly, it did not take off in the way that he or I were expecting. People struggled to really get to grips with the tune and instead of launching us into worship, it felt like a bit of a false start. As far as I was concerned it was not a major problem; worship continued without any other hitches and Jesus was glorified. My gut response in the moment was to celebrate the fact that my friend had been courageous in giving his song a go. It quickly became apparent that his response was very different.

Almost immediately after worship finished and my friend left the stage, he texted me to apologise for what had happened. He acknowledged that his song had not worked, and he assured me that he would not do it again in the second meeting so that worship would be better. I am all for going after excellence in our serving, but I am also really keen for the people I lead to be OK with things going wrong as they take risks in response to God. There was something about my friend's text that did not sit right with me. It felt like his response was rooted in fear rather than freedom; a desire to please man through his performance over and above a desire to please God through his obedience.

I got some time with the worship leader in between services to debrief from the first meeting and talk about his text. He was quick to apologise again that his song had not worked, but I stopped him mid-sentence. I wanted to help him see what had happened from a different perspective. I asked if he felt like God had spoken to him about doing his song that morning; whether he had taken a risk and given it a go in a desire to be obedient to God. My friend answered yes to my questions. I told this gifted worship leader that I was celebrating his choice to be obedient and take a risk over and above the outcome of his obedience. I then told him that God was celebrating the same thing. God is so much more interested in what is going on in our hearts than the result of what we do for Him.

I learned a valuable lesson that morning. I realised that if I want to make space for the people I lead to flourish, I need to teach them that God's measure of success is obedience. I need to model to them that the choice to be obedient to God is more important than the outcome of the obedience. If my worship-leading friend had not had his definition of success redefined that morning he probably would have thought twice about taking a risk with one of his songs again. The trouble with that is, if you stop taking risks you stop growing. You ultimately become limited and restricted by your own ability because your focus is on what you can do in your own strength rather than what God is able to do through you.

On the flip side, if you understand the truth that God is looking for and celebrating obedience irrespective of the outcome, you can say yes to things that are way beyond your natural capabilities and not be held back by fear. You can take risks and step out of your comfort zone knowing that whether things turn out brilliantly or take a nosedive, God is already well pleased with you. Our responsibility is the obedience; God's responsibility is the outcome. The exciting thing is that when we live in this place of prioritising obedience over performance, we live with a continual awareness of our complete dependence on God. When we live dependent on God we are able to see and do things that are not possible apart from Him.

## GOD LOVES OBEDIENCE

Obedience is important to God; it is a big deal to Him. When we are obedient to God, both in obeying the commands He lays out in Scripture and responding to His prompts and nudges on a day-to-day basis, we demonstrate our love for Him. Jesus told His disciples, 'You are my friends if you do what I command' (John 15:14). Our obedience pleases the heart of God. It shows Him that He has first place in our lives, and that what He wants for us and what He says to us is more important than anything else. Our obedience demonstrates to God that we are more than just His disciples, we are His friends.

Jesus regularly taught His disciples about the importance of obedience and taking risks. He knew that if He could strip them of self-reliance and instead train them to be dependent on the Father like He was, then anything would be possible. The disciples' dependence on God and their obedience to Him were crucial if they were to be all He had called them to be and have the influence they were commissioned to have. In order to train His disciples, Jesus often put them in situations that meant they were out of their depth, where their only option was to learn to rely on God.

The feeding of the 5,000 started with the disciples encouraging Jesus to send the crowds away because it was getting late and they did not have anything to eat. Jesus told them that was not necessary. 'They do not need to go away. You give them something to eat' (Matthew 16:14). The disciples did not yet understand what was possible through obedience and dependence on God, but Jesus allowed them to participate in an astonishing food-multiplying miracle. The abundance of food left over must have been a massive eye-opener for the disciples. When you look to God and lean on Him, you do not just receive enough to get by, you receive so much more than you need. Anything is possible with God.

When Jesus sent the disciples out to proclaim the Kingdom of God and to heal the sick, He sent them with this instruction, 'Do not take a purse or bag or sandals' (Luke 10:4). Jesus' aim at the point of releasing His disciples to 'do the stuff' was to reinforce the importance of dependence on their Father and being obedient to Him. When they came back celebrating that demons were submitting to them, the outcome of their obedience, Jesus redirected their celebration to the fact that they were friends of God. 'Do not rejoice that the spirits submit to you, but rejoice that your names are written in heaven' (Luke 10:20). Jesus pointed to the reason for the disciples' obedience, that they were known by God and had relationship with Him. Our obedience to God flows out of us knowing Him and who He says we are.

God loves it when we are dependent on Him. I think that is why when He asks us to be obedient it often requires us to walk through fear and take risks. The bigger the risk the greater the dependence, and the greater the dependence the greater the potential for God to break in. Our motivation for taking risks and being obedient should be first and foremost to bring glory to God. When we do what He says, when we make His agenda for our lives more important than our own, we point to Him. When we lay our lives down to serve the poor, when we apologise with humility to the person we upset, when we give our money sacrificially to build the church, God is glorified. The amazing thing about obedience is that as we lay our lives down to make much of Jesus, we end up discovering who we have been made to be. God is a loving Heavenly Father who wants the best for us. He has plans to prosper us, to draw the best out of us and to use us to have a significant impact on the earth. Our 'yes' empowers us to be everything He has called us to be. 'Whoever finds their life will lose it, and whoever loses their life for my sake will find it' (Matthew 10:39).

If we want to be leaders who see those we lead succeed, we need to understand that success in the Kingdom looks like obedience. I am not saying that we should never focus on performance. A key part of our role as leaders is to train and equip people we are investing in to grow in their gifts and abilities. What I am saying is that a person's performance must never become more important than their choice to be obedient. Whether someone does something brilliantly or it all goes horribly wrong, our first question to them, before we talk about how they could grow, should be, 'Did you do everything God asked you to do?' When we celebrate obedience over performance we empower those we lead to take risks and grow in dependence on God. This kind of leadership is only possible when we are secure in our identity as sons and daughters.

## BARRIERS TO OBEDIENCE

In order to encourage those we lead to make obedience to God the top priority in their lives, we need to train and equip them to recognise His voice when He speaks to them. If people cannot recognise what God is saying to them, they cannot do what He says. It is important that we teach people how to interpret God's Word so that they understand what obedience to Him looks like through Scripture. It is also important that we equip people to recognise the 'rhema' word of God in their lives, the way God speaks to them through the Holy Spirit 'in the moment'. A believer who is taught to recognise and respond to the voice of God is an empowered believer. Yet promoting obedience to God can pose a challenge to leaders who are not secure in their identity.

If you lead as an orphan you might struggle to promote people's obedience to God in a few ways. You might avoid equipping people to tune into and respond to God's voice because you are more interested in them being obedient to you than being led by Him. If we are not secure in our identity as sons and daughters, we are likely to look to the people around us to make us feel good about ourselves. When those we lead follow us and are obedient to us, we will feel affirmed and valued. If we are not careful we may fall into the temptation of wanting people to focus more on us and our agenda rather than pointing them to the Father and what He has for them.

I have friends who have felt God clearly speak to them about moving towns to join a different church, but have met with resistance from their church leaders when they have met to talk it through. On some occasions these friends have felt bad about trying to be obedient to God. Rather than being open-handed and releasing, their leaders have emphasised all the reasons why they should stay. Of course, as leaders it is important that we give wise counsel to those we invest in and that we ask them good questions to help them make decisions. However, there is a difference between giving counsel that leaves people feeling empowered to choose and counsel that leaves them feeling controlled. In some cases, the people we lead may well have misheard. Prioritising people's obedience to God does not mean we have to be totally hands-off as leaders. In these instances we can be honest with people about our concerns while at the same time trusting God to redirect them and cover their mistakes. Ultimately, our job is to point people to God and champion their desire to be obedient to Him. It is God's job to do the rest.

If you are not secure in your identity you may also find it difficult to celebrate people's obedience to God because the reality is that it can be messy. God loves to call us to things that are beyond our natural capabilities. If you are leading as an orphan, much of your identity will be wrapped up in your own and others' performance. Your focus will be on managing how the people you lead perform so that you can make a good impression on your peers and superiors. Insecure leaders tend to be risk-averse because if everything goes pear-shaped it reflects badly on them; they like to play it safe. The trouble with this is that God loves to ask us to do things that feel risky so that we learn to depend on Him. Insecure leaders often prefer to have everything clearly mapped out in advance, yet generally you cannot know how your obedience is going to play out until you take the first step.

Take Ananias' story, for example. God told him in a vision to go to Saul, a Pharisee who was ordering the death of Christians, to pray for him so that his sight could be restored. The request seemed absurd. Why would Ananias put his life at risk by willingly going to a man who was murdering Christians? There was no way for Ananias to know the outcome of his obedience should he choose to go, and I am pretty sure if I was mentoring him through the whole thing my wise counsel would have been for him to stay at home: 'You must be hearing wrong, Ananias.'

Yet Ananias decided to take the risk. He wrestled with God for a moment but chose to let obedience and dependence override his fear. Ananias' encounter with Saul in Acts 9 led to Saul being filled with the Holy Spirit and baptised, and the rest is history. One man's obedience to God led to the transformation of another man who is still one of the most significant influencers in the church worldwide. Not everything God asks us to do is easy or comfortable. I think we can sometimes assume that God likes to play things as safe as we do, interpreting extreme risk as reckless and inadvisable. Yet when I think about my heroes of the faith who have had massive Kingdom influence on the earth, all of them have said yes to things that I would probably have deemed unwise. God loves it when we are dependent on Him. As secure sons and daughters, it is key that we champion and celebrate the risks that those we develop take in obedience to God. You just never know what their 'yes' will lead to.

If your identity is in your performance, the possible flip side to being risk-averse is pushing the people you lead into taking risks that they are not comfortable with. In your desire to impress people, you might put those you lead in vulnerable positions so that they can perform on your behalf. The trouble with this is that it can damage people rather than enabling them to flourish, because they feel unsafe and exposed. The focus is still about their obedience to you so that you can fulfil your agenda, rather than promoting their obedience to God.

I remember taking a team on a ministry trip where I did this to a girl I was investing in. I was speaking at a women's conference and as part of the day I wanted to get the ladies walking through fear so that they could step into freedom. I was eager to impress because a lady who used to disciple me was in the room; I wanted to show her how much I had grown since she had moved away. I decided to get the ladies to sing prophetically over each other and, without giving her any warning, asked my friend to come up to the front to demonstrate how to do it in front of everyone. I had total confidence that she would be able to do what I was asking, but I had not taken into account how scary she would find the whole thing.

Honestly, my friend's prophetic song was amazing. She ended up repeating some things the lady she was singing over had recently written in her journal. Yet the impressive outcome that boosted my ego was definitely not worth the ordeal I put my friend through. She has since had to pray through the pain and fear of that moment. Putting her on the spot like that did not cause her to flourish, in fact it wounded her and shattered her confidence. I have apologised many times since that day and have never made the same mistake again. Of course, it is good for us as leaders to encourage those we are developing to take risks: that is often how they will grow. Ultimately our aim should be their obedience to God over and above obedience to us. As we encourage those around us to take risks, we must be really sure that they feel safe and covered by us and that they always have the option to say no if something feels too much.

## NAVIGATING MISTAKES

As we promote and prioritise obedience to God, mistakes will be made. One of the main ways I have learned to recognise what God is saying to me is by being obedient to what I think He has said and then seeing if I was right. I have been wrong many times, but my mistakes have helped me to tune into God's voice with greater clarity. Mistakes help us to grow. When people we lead take risks in obedience to God, they are likely to get some things wrong. It is vital that we are there to champion their obedience, irrespective of the outcome. It is also crucial that we cover them and help them navigate any mess or embarrassment they experience so that they keep choosing to take risks in the future.

Of course, in some instances people think they are being obedient to God when in reality they are misrepresenting Him. On these occasions it is important that we challenge those we lead and make the most of the opportunity to disciple them; to help them grow in their sonship or daughterhood. At times people may use 'obedience to God' as a justification for their ungodly behaviour. Maybe in a moment of heightened emotion they convince themselves they are being obedient to God when in actual fact their behaviour goes against what He stands for. This makes me think of Simon Peter who, in his desire to protect Jesus when He was about to be arrested, struck the servant of the high priest and cut off his ear. Thankfully I have not yet had to deal with someone I have responsibility for wielding a weapon and maiming a government official's aide! We can learn a lot from Jesus' response. He rebuked Peter sternly but then covered his mistake by healing the servant's ear. Peter's error was not a deal-breaker for Jesus, it was an opportunity for discipleship. Peter was still called to have massive influence.

Often mistakes are made when the people we champion take risks in a genuine attempt to be obedient to God. I remember taking a team to a church and encouraging them to prophesy over people from the front as part of the meeting. A guy on my team felt like he heard from God for an elderly couple sitting a few rows from the back, so he asked them both to stand up as he shared what he felt God had said. I caught a few anxious glances from people who knew them around the room and it soon became clear why. Maybe a minute into sharing the prophetic word, my friend decided he should probably check that this elderly lady and gentleman were actually together. Very quickly the answer came back that they were just friends.

It would have been very easy for this team member to completely backtrack and cave under the tangible awkwardness in the room. Instead, we all laughed and my friend proceeded to prophesy over both the lady and the gentleman as individuals. I was so proud of how he handled the whole thing. My role as his leader in this instance was to remind him that God's measure of success was his obedience and to celebrate the fact that he had taken a risk. My friend did not need any help in knowing what he could do differently next time he prophesied. I imagine he will always check that people are actually together before he starts prophesying over couples in the future.

The wonderful thing about creating a culture where people are equipped and empowered to be obedient to God is that you get to witness people coming alive as they step into all God has for them. You get to see people influencing their workplaces, schools, families and communities as they learn to depend on God and draw on His resources. You also get those spine-tingling moments when a person's obedience leads to stunning breakthrough. I have had the privilege of witnessing many of these moments but one in particular stands out in my mind.

Our TSM students were heading onto the streets one Saturday to bless Bedford. One of the team leaders approached me after the morning teaching session to ask if he could take his team to the hospital. He had felt God speak to him about going there and a member of his team had felt the same thing. I was slightly reluctant. We did not want to be at the hospital uninvited, and yet it did seem like God was speaking. I agreed to let the team go, but encouraged them to be sensitive about who they spoke to and to avoid going on the wards.

When the students returned to share stories a few hours later we had the joy of celebrating an incredible encounter at the hospital. Two ladies on the team decided to go and sit in A&E to see if God prompted them to speak to anyone. Their attention was drawn to a particular lady, so they courageously approached her and got into a conversation. This precious lady was not physically unwell, but emotionally and mentally she was really struggling. Our students had the opportunity to encourage her and speak truth to her. They were able to pray for her and tell her about Jesus. The lady later acknowledged that God must have sent our students to her that afternoon to save her life. Before our students left, they had the privilege of leading their new friend to Jesus. The lady left A&E without being seen by a doctor because she felt so much better. God had broken in!

The story continued after we all celebrated that Saturday. The lady turned up at church the next morning, still talking about how different she felt having met our students the day before. She quickly got plugged into our church community and after a few months got baptised. Jesus really did save her life that Saturday. I am so glad we took the risk of being obedient to God's promptings to go to the hospital. Sometimes our attempts to be obedient to God and the risks we take go horribly wrong. Stories like this one make all those times worth it. You just never know what might happen when you choose to say yes to Him.

## CULTURE OF OBEDIENCE

If we want to be leaders who create a culture where people prioritise being obedient to God, we have to help those we lead to feel safe taking risks. Obedience almost always involves an element of risk because it pushes us out of our comfort zones and invites us to depend on God. As leaders we have to communicate that we will champion people's choice to be obedient over what their obedience achieves. We must also demonstrate that we will support and stand by those we invest in if their attempts to be obedient do not turn out as they expect.

Maybe the most important thing for us, as we lead others into obedience, is the need for us to model living a life of obedience to God and taking risks when He prompts us to. It also really matters how we respond when the risks we take do not produce the fruit we were hoping for.

1) Model obedience and taking risks

The truth is that all of us, whether we have been in leadership for years or we are just starting out, have more to learn. None of us ever arrives. The danger for many of us in leadership is the temptation to spend so much time focusing on the people we are leading that we forget about our own journey with God and what He wants to do in us. It is easy for leaders to plateau, to take all of their risks when they first take on responsibility, but then quickly become safe and comfortable. The trouble with this is twofold. Firstly, we miss out on the growth and adventures God has for us. Secondly, we minimise obedience and risk in others because we do not show them what this kind of life looks like. Conversely, if we prioritise obedience to God in our own lives, not only do we continue to grow, we also give permission for those around us to pursue obedience and take risks too.

I remember being in a worship time at our TSM day school and God speaking to me about singing a spontaneous song. The sense I got was that my obedience to God would create space for others in the room to be obedient too. Knowing that did not make it any easier! I wrestled with God for a while. I felt unusually nervous and vulnerable about putting myself out there, but then I went for it. I sang my song to God. It was nothing special and if I did not know that God's measure of success is obedience I could have spent a long time analysing what I had sung and how it could have been better. I told the students that I felt there were others in the room who also had songs to sing. One by one the students took the opportunity to be obedient to God and take their own risk. As students stepped out of their comfort zones, many singing out for the first time, God's presence rushed to meet with us and Jesus was glorified. If we want to empower people to take risks for God, it is crucial that we model taking risks ourselves. When was the last time the people you lead saw you take a risk in response to Jesus?

## 2) Model that making mistakes is OK

Almost as important as modelling being obedient and taking risks is modelling being OK if the risks you take go wrong. If those we develop see us beating ourselves up when we make mistakes, the message they pick up will be that success is all about the outcome. If they witness us being hard on ourselves when we get things wrong, they will learn that mistakes are not OK and that if they are going to take a risk they better make sure the outcome is good. The trouble with this is that over time people who see us responding like this are likely to stop taking risks and instead choose to play it safe. The best way to teach those we invest in that making mistakes is OK, is by making mistakes and being OK!

This is something I have really had to work on. Like a lot of people I have stacks of grace for other people when they mess up, but not often the same amount of grace for myself. I have had to fight to be OK when I make mistakes because it is really important to me that the people I lead learn that God's measure of success is obedience. I want them to feel safe to take risks as they learn to be obedient to God because I know that by doing so they are going to grow and develop in Him. I have not always modelled this perfectly, but I am growing in it and have chosen to invite those I am championing to help me on the journey. Recently, a leadership group I facilitate were tasked with the responsibility of asking me if I had been kind to myself when I made a mistake. In the weeks that followed, I either made lots more mistakes than usual or I was just more aware of them. I had plenty of opportunities to work hard at responding to myself with kindness rather than criticism. Slowly but surely my orphan thinking is giving way to my identity in Christ. I am learning not just to teach that God's measure of success is obedience, but to live it too. How about you?

Redefining success as obedience is crucial if we want the people we are investing in to flourish in God. It is also crucial if we want to see creativity flourish. I believe that God wants to increasingly release creativity in the church and in the marketplace. When people feel free to express themselves through creativity, God is revealed because He is *the* Creator. Paintings, dance, poems and plays all have the potential to display something of the nature and character of God. I believe God wants to reveal Himself more and more to people who do not know Him through the arts and through media. In order for this to happen, believers across the world need to be empowered and released to create. If that is going to happen these believers need to feel safe.

Creativity makes us vulnerable and requires a lot of risk. As Christians create in response to God's promptings, things are not going to be immediately perfect. Creativity takes time and a lot of trial and error. Lessons are learned as people take risks and give things a go. At King's Arms we enjoy a lot of creativity. Artists paint throughout worship, sometimes people dance and we even once had someone bring a rap as a contribution. We have people who write songs, blogs and scripts for plays, for both inside and outside the church. We have interior designers and photographers, and one of our groups makes quilts to give away to charity. These are only the people I know about personally. In a church of over a thousand there will be so much more creativity that I am not even aware of.

When people create, there is a process; the first draft becomes the second and so on until what is being created evolves into what it is meant to be. Creativity will not flourish in a performance-driven culture. In order to release creativity in our churches and workplaces, we have to teach people that success is in their obedience. We have to celebrate the risks that people take and create space for them to try new things without fear of being judged or ridiculed. I believe that God loves creativity. In order for us to promote it as leaders, we must redefine people's understanding of success as obedience. The level of creativity in your church or workplace, or even your family could be a helpful indicator as to how much people have really grasped this truth.

God's measure of success is obedience. He loves it when we are obedient to Him because it shows that we love Him. He also loves it because it requires us to depend on Him, and when Christians learn to depend on God anything is possible. As leaders our job is to champion people's obedience to God. We have the privilege of creating a culture where obedience is celebrated over outcome and risks are more important than reputation. As we provide a safe place for people to step out of their comfort zones, we also have the privilege of seeing them experience the joy of learning to lean on God and see Him come through for them.

How are you doing at training and equipping those you lead to recognise and respond to God's voice?

Are you pointing people around you to the Father, rather than wanting them to focus on you and your agenda?

Do people feel safe to make mistakes when you are in the room?

Obedience to God is not always easy and it can sometimes be messy. Yet the potential fruit of a life fully submitted to the Father far outweighs any mistakes made along the way. Jesus has promised us 'life in all its fullness' (John 10:10, TLB). I think obedience is key if we want this truth to be realised in our lives. In the words of the hugely inspiring Jackie Pullinger, 'You can't lose if you put yourself completely in God's hands.'[14]

# 9. LEAVE A LEGACY

It was time to listen out for the applause of heaven.

A year after I passed on the leadership of TSM, Marco and the team were building well together, the school was growing and God still had His hand on everything going on. I was still connected to TSM and the team, functioning in more of a coaching role and being present as a mother in the school to bring my unique gifts and contributions. It was such a joy to see the team adapt to new leadership with only a few road bumps to navigate along the way. It was also a real encouragement to see Marco grow in confidence as he stepped into the role of team leader. Mostly the leadership transition was very smooth. Yet I would be lying if I said there were no more orphan-versus-daughterhood tussles to work through in my heart.

I remember one tussle, which happened at our TSM launch weekend. Marco was up the front welcoming our wide-eyed and expectant students and I was at the back of the room familiarising myself with new faces. As Marco went on to share the vision of the school, the students welcomed him and what he said with great honour and enthusiasm. All eyes were on Marco as the leader and vision-setter of the school. It should have been a moment of pride and celebration for me. I had done what Jesus had asked me to do. I had passed on leadership of TSM and now Marco was being well received to lead things forward. Yet amidst snippets of internal celebration, I found myself quite unexpectedly feeling jealous, surplus to requirements and invisible.

It is difficult to really know how much identity and sense of worth you get from what you do until you stop doing it. It is also hard to know how much affirmation and security you get from people looking to you for leadership until they start looking to someone else. God used this moment to highlight some orphan thinking in my life. He showed me where I was getting my value from other people and what I did rather than Him. The internal tussle began. The orphan part of me had a strong desire to leave the room because I made the assumption I was no longer needed. Yet my mothering instincts knew I was bringing strength to Marco and the team just by being present and available. My orphan heart experienced the pain of no longer being the centre of people's attention and the one they looked to for leadership. As a daughter of a good Father, I knew that being out of sight at the back of the room rather than being seen at the front took nothing away from my value and identity. It was time to listen out for the applause of heaven.

God spoke to me really clearly in the midst of the tussle. As my true identity wrestled with the orphan responses trying to take root in my mind, God reminded me that my reward is in heaven. Through a gentle internal whisper that strengthened and comforted me, God encouraged me to look up, to take my eyes off of the situation in front of me and to focus instead on His smile. I took a moment while Marco was still speaking to listen for my Father's 'well done'. As I closed my eyes and looked at Him, I quickly felt His affirmation and delight flood over me. I was able to connect with God's joy over me, and His joy over what I had done. God took great pleasure in my obedience to give away something so important to me, something that brings so much life change and Kingdom impact. In that moment, when it was just me and my Father, I realised this is what leadership is all about. I had given away for free something I had paid a price for, which set Marco up for great success. This is now part of my legacy.

## JESUS' LEGACY

Jesus left a legacy that every believer on the planet is partaking in right now. We get for free what He paid the ultimate price for and it sets us up for great success. Jesus knew if He could train His disciples to think like He thought and do the stuff He did they would change the world around them. Jesus' focus during the disciples' three years with Him was to get them ready for when He went back to heaven. He taught them that God was their Father and He showed them how to pray; He challenged their unbelief and exposed their self-reliance; He equipped them to heal the sick and He taught them the importance of serving in order to be great in the Kingdom. Every moment was an opportunity to highlight orphan thinking and empower His disciples to think and live like sons and daughters. When the commission came to 'make disciples of all nations' (Matthew 28:19) and the disciples received the promised Holy Spirit (Acts 2), there was no stopping the gospel.

Disciples are still making disciples today and good news is still being preached to the poor. The Kingdom of God is still being proclaimed and demonstrated all over the world, the sick are getting healed and the spiritually oppressed set free. The lonely are still being welcomed into family and sons and daughters are still relating to God as their Father. Jesus' death and resurrection, the legacy He left, means that the Holy Spirit is still being poured out, which ensures believers are set up for great success. What amazes me is that although we cannot add anything to the legacy Jesus left us (when He declared on the cross 'it is finished'[15] He really meant it), we are invited to co-labour with Him and what He is doing on the earth. As sons and daughters of God, we get to inherit for free what Jesus won for us and then pay our own price to see His rule and His reign go further and wider than it's been before.

Any legacy we leave flows out of the ultimate legacy Jesus left, He is the source of it all and all the glory goes to Him. Yet that does not mean our lives are insignificant or that we should not be intentional about leaving a spiritual legacy of our own. If we can follow Jesus' example and be deliberate about empowering, equipping and releasing others to think like Jesus and do what He did, we will see amazing Kingdom breakthrough across our towns and cities. Sons and daughters want to see the people around them fully alive and free so they succeed in whatever God calls them to. They recognise the potential of investing in other people and understand that when they speak truth to someone it draws the best out of them. Sons and daughters are eager to give people around them space and permission to take risks because they realise this could be the catalyst they need to step into God's purpose for their life. Imagine churches, workplaces and families filled with secure sons and daughters who are all focused on strengthening and releasing the people around them. Unstoppable!

Do you know what kind of legacy you want to leave? Personally I am passionate about seeing believers get revelation of who God is as their Father, who they are as His dearly loved sons and daughters and what they carry. When Christians grasp how loved they are and that God actually lives inside them and wants to flow through them, they start to realise the significance of what they are called to. I love to spot people who have caught a glimpse of God's heart for something and then get time with them to encourage them and help them work out what their next steps could be. I remember doing that once with a lady who felt passionate about raising awareness of the need for adoption and fostering within Christian families. I met with her for an hour a month for about year. I listened to her, encouraged her, spoke truth to her when she was hearing lies and helped her put together a plan of possible next steps to bring change. This lady is now a local champion for Home for Good,[16] adoption Sunday is part of our church calendar because of her influence, and families in the church are considering the part they can play. Only God knows the number of children whose lives will be transformed because of her leadership. I love knowing that I played a small part in the legacy she will leave.

More recently I have had the joy of connecting with a lady doing TSM who is a general practitioner. She has caught something of God's desire to be involved with her work, so she is learning to ask Him for solutions when she struggles to know the next step for a patient. God is giving her words of knowledge to bring breakthrough. On one occasion when she met with a patient suffering with severe mental health issues, God told her to ask him about what happened in his life when he was five. During his consultation the patient, without any prompts from my friend, started to talk about a significant event that took place in his life when he was a child. My GP friend knew that this life-defining event was key to her patient's recovery because God had told her about it as she had prayed the night before. My friend was able to draw up a plan with her patient for him to take to his psychiatrist so they could hone in on what happened when he was five. A situation that seemed to be stuck where there was little hope was changed because a GP learning to be a daughter realised her Dad has all the answers.

I have only met with this lady a few times. She tells me her stories as I sit wide-eyed at her courage, and I encourage her and speak truth to her. As a result of one of our meetings, we are now investigating a potential opportunity to serve our local emergency department. I know this woman is called to have serious influence, in the healthcare sector and also wider than that. She is carrying a fire in her belly to see God's Kingdom advance on the earth; all I am trying to do is blow on the flames and cheer her on as she runs her race. Only God knows the number of patients and healthcare professionals who will be impacted as my friend keeps being obedient to Jesus. I am sure I will be increasingly gobsmacked by the stories she shares. I feel so privileged to play a very small part in the wonderful legacy she will leave.

What legacy will you leave? Maybe you will see women and children who are caught up in sex trafficking experience freedom and be reinstated with dignity into society. Maybe you will see the gospel impact the rich and famous as you walk through open doors in the entertainment industry. Maybe you will see marriages strengthened and families restored, or maybe your legacy is about seeing the lonely and broken in your community find hope and liberty as you speak truth to them and pray with them. Whatever God has put in your heart regarding the influence you are called to have, go for it! Find others who share the same passions as you, encourage them and create space for them to succeed in the influence they are called to have. The Kingdom impact we can see through empowering those around us is so much greater than what is possible on our own. And when God calls you to give away something you love that you have worked hard to build so that those coming after you can flourish, do it willingly. Remember this is part of your legacy too.

## RAISE AND RELEASE SONS AND DAUGHTERS

Secure sons and daughters make the best fathers and mothers. They know what it looks and feels like to be parented in a healthy way. It is very difficult to be an effective father or mother if your experience of being fathered and mothered has been non-existent or broken. A lack of fathering and mothering is what leads to orphan thinking and behaviour. If you have been influenced by orphan leadership and you struggle to fully embrace being a son or daughter, you will only be able to replicate what you know. Leaders who think and behave like orphans tend to produce more orphans, yet God's desire is that we raise up sons and daughters.

The natural trajectory for leaders who are secure in their

sonship and daughterhood is that they start to see themselves as mothers and fathers. People who learn to receive love and acceptance from the ultimate Father are able to give His love away to everyone they meet. When we lead as fathers and mothers we instinctively begin to raise up sons and daughters. Our aim intuitively becomes to empower and release the people around us to be all God has called them to be. The fruit of this kind of leadership is that our sons and daughters ultimately transition into fathers and mothers who then raise up their own secure children. This kind of Kingdom legacy just keeps multiplying because it is rooted in relationship and building family: the wineskin God always intended for His church.

The enemy is waging war against this wineskin of family. He knows the impact fathering and mothering can have on mobilising the church and advancing the Kingdom so he aims to make church families dysfunctional. His plan is to keep leaders enslaved as orphans and if they do start to think of themselves as fathers and mothers, to limit their effectiveness. I experienced this first-hand when I turned forty last year. I am single and I do not have any children of my own. During the week leading up to my birthday, the deep grief I felt about not being a mum hit me. As I wept with God and told Him again about my disappointment, I remembered I had been put on the preaching rota to speak on Mother's Day at King's Arms. March was just a few months away and the thought of preaching immediately evoked fear in me. The enemy, who is prowling around like a lion looking for people to devour (see 1 Peter 5:8), saw his chance to try to take me out. 'You can't speak on Mother's Day. You don't know what it's like to be a mum. You'd be a fraud.' This is the thought that lingered in my mind.

The most powerful lies the enemy tells us always have an element of truth in them. The truth is I cannot know what it is like to be a mum because I do not have my own children. The conclusion, however, that I would be a fraud to speak on Mother's Day was frankly a load of rubbish. I might not have my own biological children, but I have invested in and released hundreds of spiritual sons and daughters. The lie that I would be a fraud was laughable, although at the time I needed friends to help me see that. The enemy was trying to undermine my call to be a mother in the church. He wanted me to keep quiet, to take a step back and to doubt my effectiveness at raising sons and daughters because he knows the impact it has. Recognising his schemes enabled me to reject the lies and choose to keep being me. I did preach that Sunday, and as a result of the enemy's attempt to undermine me I am now more intentionally embracing my role as a mum. As a mother, my dream is to release hundreds of sons and daughters all over the world to advance God's Kingdom wherever they are. In order to do this, I need to keep investing in my own journey of growing in security as a dearly loved daughter.

The enemy not only tries to ambush the church's family wineskin by taking out individuals, he also does it by sowing division and mistrust between men and women. This is a much bigger topic than I have the ability to adequately unpack here, but I did want to share a couple of key observations, which I think are hindering some churches from building the legacy God has for them. One observation is to do with the way fathers (male leaders in the church) tend to focus on investing in and raising up sons, and mothers (female leaders in the church) tend to focus on developing and empowering daughters. If you put this blueprint for leadership development against the backdrop of healthy biological families, it makes little sense. In healthy families sons need a mother as much as they need a father, and daughters need a dad as much as they need a mum. Why then in the church do we often aspire more to a single-parent family model than the family design God intended?

I think much of this practice is birthed out of a good heart, the desire of male leaders in particular to be pure and above reproach. There have been some really tragic stories over the years of male leaders whose marriages have fallen apart because they got too close to another woman. Obviously there needs to be wisdom when fathers invest in daughters and when mothers invest in sons, but it must be a wisdom rooted in faith, not fear. Fear has resulted in many male leaders holding women at arm's length or avoiding them altogether by focusing their attention on sons. This cannot be the best solution and it certainly will not produce the most fruit.

Some men may avoid championing daughters because they believe lies similar to mine, that they don't have what it takes to father. Others may find it challenging to relate to and communicate with women so they stay within their comfort zone and only invest in sons. Some men may steer clear of developing women because the women they have tried to lead in the past have been independent and difficult. The problem with all of this is that women need men around them. They need fathers and brothers cheering them on, telling them who they are and drawing the best out of them. God designed it so the father's role in a family is to call out the identity of his children. No wonder many churches are full of fearful and insecure women who regularly question if they really have permission to be themselves. They struggle to know who they are and where they fit because no fathers are telling them. Of course, as women we ultimately need to hear the truth about our identity from our Heavenly Father, but God has put us in family so earthly fathers can play their part too.

In the same way, sons need mothers just as much as they need fathers. Men need mothers and sisters involved in their lives; provoking them, championing them and helping them to see they have what it takes. I am so grateful to have the privilege of investing in and releasing sons. At times I have had to speak truth to the guys I am leading that has been really hard to hear. I have been so impressed by their humility in receiving my challenge and their desire to grow and change. I wonder if sometimes, because of the way men and women are wired, guys find it easier to hear the truth from mothers and sisters. I love opportunities I get to help men I invest in connect with what is going on in their hearts. Women tend to be more emotionally aware then men. As we ask good questions, we can help the guys we lead to go on their own journey of growing in self-awareness and emotional intelligence. As we have already seen, this is such a key part of effective leadership. When sons have fathers *and* mothers speaking into their lives, they are so much richer for it.

My concern is that many men in the church are not looking for this kind of investment from female leaders. I think maybe because in some churches female leadership has not been valued sufficiently and has not had adequate profile. We have tended to elevate the role of fathers above mothers, and as a result sons and daughters are looking for fathering more than they are mothering. Even as I write the word 'mothering' I can feel the negative connotations of its meaning surface in my heart. It can evoke feelings of being smothered, mollycoddled and emasculated. However, mothering to me looks like the provoking, empowering and releasing leadership I have outlined in this book. Our perception of mothering in parts of the church has to be different if we are going to function as family in the way God intends us to. I love that the apostle Paul references Rufus' mother in Romans 16 as being like a mother to him. He was not averse to submitting himself as a son to a mother and receiving significant input from a woman. I am convinced that this gives us a glimpse of God's heart for the role of mothers investing in sons in the church.

My other observation is linked to the limited profile women in leadership are given in some churches. When God created Adam and Eve, He blessed them and said to them, 'Be fruitful and multiply and fill the earth and subdue it' (Genesis 1:28, ESV). In other words, God's original intention was for Adam and Eve to lead on the earth and take authority over it together, shoulder to shoulder. This is what leadership in healthy families looks like. Families flourish when fathers and mothers work together, make decisions together and shape their family together. In light of this, I find it confusing when churches only have fathers at the front on Sundays leading the family. I also struggle to understand why fathers sometimes make all the key decisions regarding the vision or future of a church without any input from mothers. This practice would make no sense in a biological family. If a father made all the decisions about what would be best for his kids and then told his wife without asking for her input, we would call it unhealthy. Families flourish most when fathers and mothers lead together. The same is true in the church.

Our ultimate aim as sons and daughters is to become fathers and mothers who raise up more sons and daughters. If we want to leave a legacy in the church we need to work towards fathers and mothers leading together. When we work together as men and women, we are able to more effectively represent the rich and multifaceted nature of God. Both men and women are made in the image and likeness of God. This means if we only promote and release men and not women, or if we only champion and develop women and not men, we miss out on revelation of Him. When fathers and mothers lead together we get a more complete glimpse of what God is like, and those we invest in benefit from being released in a healthy family. How are you doing at seeing yourself as a father or mother in your leadership? Are both fathers and mothers seen, released and part of the decision-making process in your church family or sphere of influence? Are the people you are championing benefiting from the input of both fathers and mothers? Raising and releasing sons and daughters in a family wineskin[17] carries so much potential. When we are intentional about pointing those we lead to the ultimate Father, suddenly anything is possible.

## LEGACY THROUGH PRAYER

Our prayers are powerful and effective: they change us, the people around us and ultimately they impact the entire planet. When

Jesus taught His disciples to pray, He instructed them to come to God as their Father. We must do the same. When we pray, we fix our eyes on the Father and remind ourselves of our complete dependence on Him. We also point those we lead to the Father, modelling to them that dependence on Him is where success lies. When our prayers are rooted in our identity and flow out of our security as dearly loved sons and daughters, there is no limit to the legacy we can leave. Our prayers open the door for us to influence nations we will never visit and see transformation in people we will never meet. Our prayers enable us to keep growing in our sonship or daughterhood and strengthen those we develop to be everything God has called them to be. Our prayers will continue to have an impact on the earth long after we have gone home to be with the Father. The prayers we pray are key to the legacy we ultimately leave.

We can leave a legacy through prayer by praying for ourselves. I pray for myself a lot, often because I am acutely aware of areas of weakness in my life but also because I know God has more for me. There is always more in God's Kingdom. I remember when I went on a journey of asking God to connect my heart to His so I could feel what He felt. I had discovered a big disconnect in my heart and knew I was struggling to feel and express emotions in a healthy way. Whenever I thought about it I asked God to heal my heart. The prayers I prayed were not long-winded or part of my extended time with Jesus, rather they were simple one-liners I said under my breath whenever I remembered what I wanted God to do.

God has been so faithful in answering my prayers. Although I still have more to learn about being emotionally healthy, I am in a completely different place now to where I used to be. My heart feels more alive than ever, I can feel deep pain and grief but also overwhelming joy. The wonderful thing about this transformation is the legacy I now get to leave. One of my strengths when I travel around speaking at other churches is giving people permission to feel and express emotion. I am seeing many believers start their own journey of growing in emotional health. This will be part of the legacy I leave and it all stemmed from prayers I prayed for myself.

We can also leave a legacy through prayer by praying for those we invest in. Jesus prayed for His disciples before He returned to the Father, and the apostle Paul prayed often for the churches he was investing in. My favourite prayer of Paul's is the one he prayed for the church in Ephesus:

> … that you, being rooted and grounded in love, may have strength to comprehend with all the saints what is the breadth and length and height and depth, and to know the love of Christ that surpasses knowledge, that you may be filled with all the fullness of God.
> (Ephesians 3:17-19, ESV)

I think if our prayers for those we lead focus on them receiving greater revelation of the Father's love for them, we cannot go far wrong.

The prayers we pray as leaders are powerful to bring about change in the people we influence and to open doors of opportunity for them to flourish in God. I remember many years ago when I was a youth leader having a young person in my group who was really negative about the gift of tongues. I would hear her speaking about the gift in a very antagonistic way and she was adamant she did not want it. As her leader, I was concerned. I knew how powerful the gift of tongues was and I wanted this girl to realise she should eagerly desire any gift the Father wanted to give because it would be good for her. I decided to have a conversation with this young person, but was unsure how to approach it so that she felt provoked but not controlled. I asked Jesus to help me and started to pray that He would change this beautiful girl's heart regarding the gift.

A week or two passed before I was able to connect with her, but when I did her mindset had already completely changed. In fact, she had started to speak in tongues! When I questioned this girl about the turnaround she told me about a dream she had where she was standing in front of the Father speaking in a new language. When she woke up she decided God must already have given her the gift of tongues and that He must want her to use it, so she did. My very brief prayers led to this young lady having an encounter with the Father in her dream, which changed her mindset and impacted her relationship with Him. The prayers we pray are powerful and effective. Sometimes we will see first-hand the impact they have in the people around us. Other times the prayers we pray will feed into and shape a legacy we will not see this side of heaven. A legacy that will only be fully realised in the generations who come after us. Either way, when secure sons and daughters pray to a perfect Heavenly Father, anything is possible. How are you doing at leaving a legacy with your prayers, both in your own life and the lives of those you have the privilege of investing in? The key for us is that we heed Jesus' encouragement to keep praying 'and not give up' (Luke 18:1).

Jesus came to change the world, to usher in a new era where His rule and reign pushed back the influence and kingdom of the enemy. He came as a son in right relationship with His Father. Sonship was what He modelled to those He led, and dependence on the Father was His strategy for fulfilling His mission. Jesus' training programme for His disciples was intended to root out orphan thinking and behaviour and plant seeds of sonship and daughterhood. Jesus was continually pointing His followers to the Father and teaching them to live their lives reliant on Him. When Jesus returned to heaven, the Kingdom and the church exploded because the disciples knew who and whose they were. Jesus' followers learned to lean into the Father, as they had seen Him do so often, and as a result they saw God's rule and reign break in wherever they went. The legacy Jesus left was multiplied by His disciples and it is still going strong today.

As believers and leaders we are drafted into this legacy and we have the privilege of multiplying it further. The most effective way we can do this is to follow Jesus' example. The best gift we can give the people we champion is to focus on being sons and daughters; to prioritise our own relationship with the Father. Whatever is going on inside us will come out of us to impact the people around us. The truth is, as we go on our own journey of recognising and rejecting orphan thinking we will increasingly be able to live and lead as sons and daughters. Sons and daughters who encourage the people we develop and speak the truth in love to them. Sons and daughters who readily give away responsibility to the people we invest in and who celebrate when they choose to take risks. Sons and daughters who discover the joy of empowering others.

When secure sons and daughters lead in the church, in families and in the marketplace the people they lead have so much potential to thrive. Imagine the possibilities for Kingdom impact around the world through leaders who lay their lives down to empower everyone around them. Jesus, the ultimate leader, shows us how this kind of leadership is possible. How are you doing at following His example?

If I can leave you with one thing as you continue on your leadership journey, it would be this: make it your aim in everything to remember you are a son or daughter. Take time to regularly enjoy the unconditional love and acceptance of your Heavenly Father. When we make this our top priority, everything we do flows out of us knowing who we are. When we learn to lead as dearly loved children, we will find great joy in empowering others to take hold of all the Father has for them: that is true success.

# Endnotes

1.  Attributed to Bill Johnson, but source unknown at the time of publication.

2.  Nicky & Pippa Gumbel, *Bible in One Year* App (London: Alpha International, 2016), 4th February.

3.  TSM stands for Training for Supernatural Ministry and is a nine-month course we run at King's Arms to equip people to live like Jesus. To find out more, go to www.tsmbedford.org.

4.  Peter Scazzero with Warren Bird, *The Emotionally Healthy Church: A Strategy for Discipleship that Actually Changes Lives* (Grand Rapids, MI: Zondervan, 2010), p.78.

5.  You can listen to a message I gave at King's Arms church about processing pain to the get to the promise here: www. kingsarms.org/resources/stories-and-testimonies/message/ processing-pain-to-get-to-the-promise.html.

6.  To find our more about the StrengthsFinder test – Tom Rath, *StrengthsFinder 2.0* (New York: Gallup Press, 2007).

7.  The Alpha course is an introductory course to Christianity. To find out more, visit https://alpha.org.

8.  To find out more about our culture you can listen to the preaching series we did as we launched culture with the church in 2009: www.kingsarms.org/resources/media/mes-sages/series/culture-five-ways-we-live.html.

9. You can listen to my preach here: //www.kingsarms.org/re-sources/stories-and-testimonies/message/responding-to-un-godly-leadership.html.

10. Attributed to Banning Liebscher, but source unknown at the time of publication.

11. You can find out more about Sharon's art on Facebook by searching 'Sharon Ryan Art'.

12. Stephen R. Covey, *The 7 Habits of Highly Effective People* (London: Simon & Schuster, 2004).

13. Reproduced with permission from Phil Wilthew, *Multiplying Disciples: A toolkit for learning to live like Jesus* (Milton Keynes: Malcolm Down Publishing, 2018), p.158.

14. Jackie Pullinger with Andrew Quicke, *Chasing the Dragon* (London: Hodder & Stoughton, 2001), p.22.

15. John 19:30.

16. Home for Good is a charity in the UK with a vision to find 'a home for every child who needs one'. To find out more infor-mation, visit their website: www.homeforgood.org.uk.

17. When I talk about a church wineskin I am referring to the way a church is structured and how it functions. God's inten-tion is that the church would be a family.

# Naturally Supernatural
## The Normal Christian Life

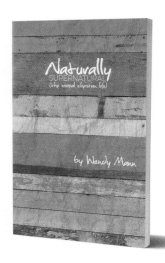

'I'd like to imagine what churches would look like if every believer realised that the life Jesus modelled is possible for them too.'
– **Wendy Mann**

The supernatural life that Jesus modelled is not reserved for a few 'superstar' Christians; it is meant to be the normal life for every believer. All Christians are called and equipped by God to see his Kingdom break in as part of their day-to-day life. Wherever they go, they can see people's lives transformed as they demonstrate God's love outside the four walls of the church.

This book unpacks over ten years of Wendy Mann's journey of learning how to live a naturally supernatural life. It is full of faith-building stories, inspiring insights and practical tools that she and her church community, King's Arms Church, Bedford, are learning along the way.

# TRAINING FOR SUPERNATURAL MINISTRY
# KINGS ARMS CHURCH, BEDFORD

The normal Christian life is about seeing God's Kingdom break out wherever we go and wherever we have influence.

TSM is a safe place to get free from the things that hold you back from living this kind of life.

Your faith will be stirred as you take risks inside the church and out on the streets.

Your courage will be built as you get equipped to bring the Kingdom of God in your day-to-day life.

TSM includes combinations of worship, teaching, activation, outreach and courage groups.

The course is open to people from any church, age or stage of life (18+).

For more information and to apply online visit:
www.tsmbedford.org